MARVIN J. ASHTON

BE OF GOOD
CHEER

BE OF GOOD CHEER

MARVIN J. ASHTON

Deseret Book Company
Salt Lake City, Utah

This book is not an official publication of The Church of Jesus Christ of Latter-day Saints, and the views expressed in it do not necessarily represent the offic:ᵌl position of the Church. The author alone is responsil its contents.

First printing October 1987
Second printing January 1988
Third printing October 1988

Library of Congress Cataloging-in-Publication Data

Ashton, Marvin J., 1915–
    Be of good cheer.

    Includes index.
    1. Spiritual life–Mormon authors.   I. Title.
BX8656.A825   1987   252'.09332   87-22357
ISBN 0-87579-106-9

Contents

Acknowledgments

Appreciation is expressed to the following:

Ronald A. Millett, Eleanor Knowles, Jack Lyon, Richard Erickson, and other members of the Deseret Book staff who helped to edit, design, and prepare this book for publication, and

Valoy Eaton, a personal friend whose fine work I admire and who has given permission for the use of one of his paintings on the dust jacket.

1
"Be of Good Cheer"

"Wherefore, be of good cheer, and do not fear,
for I the Lord am with you, and will stand by
you."

(D&C 68:5.)

Recently I have been strongly impressed to share some thoughts about the Lord's invitation to "be of good cheer"—yes, to be of good cheer without fear. With world conditions of riots, protests, arms build-ups, wars and rumors of war, mistrust, poverty, disappointments, terrorism, tragedies, and so on, there has never been a period in history when there is a greater need to accept another of the Lord's eternal promises: "Behold, this is the promise of the Lord unto you, O ye my servants. Wherefore, be of good cheer, and do not fear, for I the Lord am with you, and will stand by you; and ye shall bear record of me, even Jesus Christ, that I am the Son of the living God, that I was, that I am, and that I am to come." (D&C 68:5-6.)

Good cheer is a state of mind or mood that promotes happiness or joy. Some like to think good cheer is found in a bottle, a six-pack, an injection, a pinch under the lip, rationalization, or self-deceit. Incidentally, it has been my observation over the years that those who try to drown their sorrows with drink only sicken their tomorrows. With God's help, good cheer permits us to rise above the depressing present or difficult circumstances. It is a process of positive reassurance and reinforcement. It is sunshine when clouds block the light.

Recently, while visiting with a wife who had suddenly lost her husband through a tragic death, I was touched by this lovely lady from Washington, Utah, when she said, "My heart is heavy and sad, but my soul is of good cheer." There was a powerful inward cheer dominating the sorrowful situation. The promise "for I the Lord am with you" was triumphing over heartache and despair. People of good cheer soften the sorrows of others as well as those that weigh mightily upon themselves.

None of us will escape tragedy and suffering. Each of us will probably react differently. However, if we can recall the Lord's promise "for I the Lord am with you," we will be able to face our problems with dignity and courage. We will find the strength to be of good cheer instead of becoming resentful, critical, or defeated. We will be able to meet life's unpleasant happenings with clear vision, strength, and power.

All over the world we have many members who are taking the blessings of the gospel to those who will listen. Those who accept and live the teachings of our Savior find the strength to be of good cheer, for He declared, "Whosoever will save his life shall lose it: and whosoever will lose his life for my sake shall find it." (Matthew 16:25.) When we apply this principle in our lives and share it with our associates, it is possible to supplant discouragement, tragedy, and gloom with hope and cheer. The fruits of cheerfulness lie within each of us, side by side with our resolution, priorities, and desires. They will never come from without. They cannot be purchased or stolen. They are above price.

When I think of those about us who are well-disciplined

and anxiously engaged in being of good cheer, many great examples come to mind. They lift us with their state of mind of gladness, joy, and hope. They seem to move forward happily with an extra dimension of power and love. Let me share an example or two.

One beautiful "good cheer" lady I have loved deeply over the years is very special. For more than thirty-five years her husband has been afflicted with Parkinson's disease.

They have raised six outstanding children. She has cheerfully cooperated in making it possible for him to function well as a father, husband, bishop, high councilor, and successful building contractor. When his mobility has reached discouraging stages of near zero, she has lifted him. Her neighbors, and they are everyone she knows, find her to be the first visitor when there is an unusual need. Her good cheer is endless. She brings peace of mind and comfort to all with whom she associates. The more I watch her, the more I realize good cheer builds contagious enthusiasm.

What a joy it is to see someone of good cheer, who, when others because of an unpleasant happening or development live in angry silence or vocal disgust, meets the situation with cheerful endurance and good spirits.

Our missionaries worldwide frequently have contacts who would be willing to accept baptism and the gospel of Jesus Christ, but who fear the process. Many are afraid to change. Other less active members of the Church resist the invitation to come back because they fear being incompatible in His paths and with new associates.

We remind all to not fear and to be of good cheer because the Son of the living God, even Jesus Christ, shall stand by you.

Just a few weeks ago, while in Bangkok, Thailand, our hearts were touched by a young lady now living in a state of good cheer she never realized was possible. Meaningful change has brought great joy and happiness to her and

her family. Let me share this message of good cheer as
told in her own words: "In 1975 there was a family who
lived near the main road in a small village. My parents
were rather poor. My father worked at the local post office,
while my mother stayed home caring for the children.

"As time passed by, my mother became bored with
her life as a housewife and set out to find a more exciting
way of life. She turned to drink, tobacco, and gambling.
Many times she would play cards all day and all night and
not return to care for her children.

"Meanwhile, my father was working hard to support
his family. Things at home were not going well, and many
times my father and my mother would argue violently.

"One day my father came home and told my mother
that if she continued on with her gambling and didn't care
for the children, he would have to divorce her. The family
faced a crisis. At that time I was helping care for my three
younger brothers. My parents asked each child who he or
she wanted to live with, Mom or Dad. It was a very difficult
decision to have to choose between my mother and my
father. It was a time of much suffering and sorrow.

"It was during this time that my oldest sister first met
some missionaries from The Church of Jesus Christ of Latter-day Saints. She studied about the Church and came to
accept the teachings and adopt them into her life. She asked
me to go to church with her. I was very sad and angry at
first to think she had changed religions. I had only known
the teachings of Buddha and had come to love the customs.

"But I noticed a change in my sister. She was more
loving and kind and did many things to help our family.
I decided to study with the missionaries. My mother listened also. Before very long, we both realized that we had
done things wrong and needed to change our lives. We
repented of our sins and were baptized. When my father
and two older brothers saw the change in us, they decided
to study also. My father had been an important officer and
teacher in the Buddhist church. He spent much time study-

ing and reading the Standard Works. He prayed often and sincerely to know the truth. At last his humble prayers were answered. He knew, as we did, that The Church of Jesus Christ of Latter-day Saints was true.

"The true gospel changed our lives and restored happiness to a nearly devastated home and family. We are all very grateful and happy to now be a part of the Lord's church and become familiar with and obey His commandments."

Today this young lady is a missionary for the Church. She and her family are living witnesses that when people come to realize that "I the Lord am with you, and will stand by you," a whole family can change their despair to good cheer.

In contrast to this family in Bangkok, some of us who have the happiness and good cheer of the gospel can lose it by becoming involved in iniquity and deceit. One of the most destructive forms of deceit is self-deceit.

Modern-day prophets have pled in plainness for us to avoid "get-rich-quick" schemes if we would avoid the heartaches of financial bondage. Perhaps we have not said enough about the fact that too many of us, in our moments of dreaming of grandeur, plant the seeds of economic disaster. Then at a later date when much is lost, we blame those who participated with us. It is difficult to be of good cheer when self-deceit is our companion. When we willingly expose ourselves to the winds and storms of fraud and scam, we should not be surprised when we come down with deficit disease. Over the years of listening to those who have suffered heavy money losses, I have heard many in desperation declare, "I was taken." Often my heart, mind, and the Spirit have prompted me to share, "Yes, you were taken by yourself." We all need to be encouraged to lift up our heads and see where our thoughts and undeclared priorities are taking us. Self-deceit permits us to blame others for our failures.

For many years President Ezra Taft Benson has reinforced his talks of love and guidance to our youth with the truth that wickedness never can be happiness. (See Alma 41:10.) In dating and courting, decisions of conduct, to be effective, must be made before the moment of enticement and temptation surfaces. Too often immoral conduct results from self-deceit. We have allowed ourselves to blame others for the incident of misconduct when our failure to make decisions ahead of time was not thought to be of importance. The thought that wickedness brings good cheer makes reason stare.

A constant effort must be made to lift our daily conduct so that it squares with our knowledge of truth and our standards. Self-mastery must always triumph over self-deceit for us to taste the fruits of good cheer.

One form of self-deceit is rationalization. We prevent the Lord from being with us because we stray from His paths and explain our actions by consciously or unconsciously making excuses. We say to ourselves, "I did it just to see what it was like." "Everyone else was doing it." "I didn't want to be different." "There was no other way to be accepted graciously." Or "He made me do it."

The companionship of good cheer is possible through keeping the commandments of God, not through rationalization. We must commit ourselves to principles and not live by comparison or excuses. Horace Mann wisely said, "In vain do they talk of happiness who never subdued an impulse in obedience to a principle." (From *Common School Journal,* quoted in *Horace Mann: His Ideas and Ideals,* comp. Joy Elmer Morgan [Washington, D.C.: National Home Library Foundation, 1936], p. 149.)

Self-deceit is at best only temporarily successful. Then when the gap between truth and our knowledge of the right and our behavior becomes too large, we are forced to close it with rationalization. The true test is, how do we measure up when Christlike conduct standards are applied.

Cheerfulness will never be a blending of self-deceit and

rationalization. Being of good cheer permits us to rise above the moment and situation. Generally, rationalization is unconscious. We slip into it unaware and gradually. It becomes a crutch for those who choose to walk in crooked paths.

The major responsibility for good cheer lies with the individual.

Good cheer is best shared by those who will discard fear, cheerfully accept what comes and use it wisely, become converted, obey the commandments of God, avoid self-deceit and rationalization.

Being of good cheer makes it possible for us to turn all of our sunsets into sunrises. With good cheer, carrying our cross can be our ladder to happiness. When Jesus comes into our lives, cheer lights the way. How powerful and comforting is the Savior's declaration, "In the world ye shall have tribulation: but be of good cheer; I have overcome the world." (John 16:33.)

He promises to stand by us. He invites us to bear record and witness of Him. What a joy and honor it is for me to declare in good cheer and without fear that Jesus Christ is the Son of the living God, that He was the Only Begotten of the Father, that He is, and that He will yet come again in God's name. I thank God for the Savior's life, His cheerful love, and His example. "There is no fear in love; but perfect love casteth out fear." (1 John 4:18.)

To all mankind everywhere I cheerfully testify that our Lord and Savior Jesus Christ is our Redeemer. He will sustain us now and forever if we will walk in His paths, be of good cheer, and not fear.

2
Pure Religion

"Pure religion and undefiled before God and the Father is this, To visit the fatherless and widows in their affliction, and to keep . . . unspotted from the world."

(James 1:27.)

A few weeks ago as I approached the temple grounds where I was to meet a friend, a young woman—a stranger to me—stepped up and said, "Would you like to know what kind of people these Mormons really are?"

I responded with, "I think I already know a little bit about what they really are."

To this the heckler retorted, "They surely don't live the teachings of Jesus Christ as they should."

My concluding comment was, "Who does?"

As I continued my walk to the visitors' center, I began to ponder the actions of those persons who are giving time and money to discredit, embarrass, ridicule, and shame those who have religious views that differ from their own. Sometimes such actions can unify and strengthen those who are attacked. However, in some few instances they plant seeds of discord, and at times righteous people are hurt by their slander.

I doubt that such actions can be called Christ-like. At no time did Jesus Christ encourage us to spend time participating in damaging, destructive criticism. His message was to encourage us to seek, learn, and share all that is praiseworthy and of value as we associate with our fellow beings. Only those who are vindictive and cantankerous participate in ferreting out and advertising the negative and unsavory.

I will be forever grateful for the wise counsel my mission president gave me as I arrived in England to serve as a missionary. He said, "Elder Ashton, these people in this land have been at it a long time. If you will keep your eyes, ears, and mind open, you can learn much while you are here. Look for the good and overlook that which is different from your ways."

The longer I stayed in England, the more I appreciated his advice. Day by day I grew to love and appreciate that great country and its people. For example, instead of freezing in the raw winter weather, I did as the English did — I put on another sweater rather than wasting time murmuring and complaining.

Robert West wrote, "Nothing is easier than fault-finding; no talent, no self-denial, no brains . . . are required to set up in the grumbling business." (*Richard L. Evans' Quote Book* [Salt Lake City, Utah: Publishers Press, 1971], p. 221.)

Whether accusations, innuendos, aspersions, or falsehoods are whispered or blatantly shouted, the gospel of Jesus Christ reminds us that we are not to retaliate nor contend. "Wherefore, my beloved brethren, let every man be swift to hear, slow to speak, slow to wrath: for the wrath of man worketh not the righteousness of God." (James 1:19-20.)

No religion, group, or individual can prosper over an extended period of time with fault-finding as their foundation. To the world, and especially to members of The Church of Jesus Christ of Latter-day Saints, we declare there is no time for contention. "If any man among you seem to be religious, and bridleth not his tongue, but deceiveth his own heart, this man's religion is vain." (James 1:26.)

The poet Robert Frost once defined education as "the ability to listen to almost anything without losing your temper or your self-confidence." Probably we will never be free of those who are openly anti-Mormon. Therefore, we encourage all our members to refuse to become anti-anti-Mormon. In the wise words of old, can we "live and let live"? (Johann Schiller, in *The Home Book of Quotations* [New York: Dodd, Mead & Company, 1935], p. 1119.)

Certainly one of our God-given privileges is the right to choose what our attitude will be in any given set of circumstances. We can let the events that surround us determine our actions—or we can personally take charge and rule our lives, using as guidelines the principles of pure religion. Pure religion is learning the gospel of Jesus Christ and then putting it into action. Nothing will ever be of real benefit to us until it is incorporated into our own lives.

It seems to me there has never been a period in history when it has been more important for us to be engaged in pure religion as taught by the Savior. This religion is not to retaliate, or to exchange in kind, evil actions or unkind statements. Pure religion encompasses the ability to cherish, to build up, and to turn the other cheek in place of destroying and tearing down. Blessed are they who strive to serve the Lord without wasting time faulting Him or those who serve Him.

The discerning realize that it is not realistic to expect perfection in others when none of us is perfect: "Why beholdest thou the mote that is in thy brother's eye, but considerest not the beam that is in thine own eye? Or how wilt thou say to thy brother, Let me pull the mote out of thine eye; and behold, a beam is in thine own eye? Thou hypocrite, first cast out the beam out of thine own eye; and then shalt thou see clearly to cast out the mote out of thy brother's eye." (Matthew 7:3-5.)

Meaningful progress can be made only when all of us can cast the motes out of our own eyes, leave judgment to our Father in heaven, and lose ourselves in righteous living.

As we reflect upon actions that do not fit the definition of pure religion, perhaps we should contemplate the nature of this term: "Pure religion and undefiled before God and the Father is this, To visit the fatherless and widows in their affliction, and to keep . . . unspotted from the world." (James 1:27.)

The words are simple, but a basic formula is revealed — namely, help those who are in need, build your life around the gospel of Jesus Christ, and avoid yielding to worldly temptations.

As with most simple formulas, all of us must analyze our own lives and use wisdom and free agency as we apply the basic principles. Jesus said, "This is my gospel; and ye know the things that ye must do in my church; for the works which ye have seen me do that shall ye also do; for that which ye have seen me do even that shall ye do." (3 Nephi 27:21.) The doing is always more difficult than the knowing.

We were visiting some friends this past summer. A very young son with a new tricycle was disturbed because his parents were giving us their attention and all of us were ignoring him. He rode his trike as fast as his little legs could pedal, calling, "Look at me!" The inevitable happened as he looked at us instead of where he was going. He rode directly into a lawn chair. To try to stem the tears and take his mind off the hurt, his mother said, "That naughty chair hurt you. Let's spank the chair." I suppose her response momentarily distracted the boy, but the mother was letting her son blame something else for the accident rather than himself. How many times do we look for something external on which to place blame for our actions? It hurts to look inward and assume responsibility for our situations.

To keep ourselves unspotted from the world requires taking charge of and ruling our lives from within, accepting responsibility for our own actions, and choosing the role of peacemaker rather than retaliator when those around us are critical or spread false propaganda. It includes being aware that God's work on earth is done by human beings, all of whom have some weaknesses. It encompasses the ability to look for the good accomplished rather than being disillusioned when human failings surface. It includes resisting the urge to proclaim such weaknesses so adamantly that the basic good is overshadowed and testimonies waver.

Pure religion is maintaining a balance between sophisticated, intellectual information and the basic "bread-and-butter" principles of the gospel. Latter-day Saints are encouraged to pursue learning in all areas. However, superior knowledge and academic achievements need to be enhanced by wisdom, good judgment, and spiritual guidance in order to use all that is learned for the benefit of the individual and his fellow beings.

Some think they can learn of God only by appreciating His handiwork. Mountains, streams, flowers, birds, and animals are to be enjoyed and admired; but this is not enough. In the formal Church setting, gospel truths are shared, new concepts are internalized, and new experiences are offered — all of which can result in enriched feelings about oneself and in learning better methods of helping others.

One who practices pure religion soon discovers it is more rewarding to lift people up than to hold them down. Happiness is bound up with helpfulness. Those who fail to protect someone's good name, who take advantage of the innocent or uninformed, who build a fortune by pretending godliness to manipulate others, are missing the joy of practicing pure religion.

Many have found joy by extending mercy and tender care to those around them. What a strength it is to witness friends visiting nursing homes to comfort patients who don't even have the capacity to express appreciation. There are some who would question God's motives when He allows many to linger in pain and hopeless physical and mental deterioration. While this process is taking place, others teach us by their compassionate service and patience. One who has served in many leadership positions in the Church, even in missions and temples, now without specific assignment, meets each month with those confined in a nursing home and often says, "What satisfaction I get each month as I visit these precious souls."

Pure religion is showing concern and affection for those who, because they have lost their companions, are experiencing feelings of loneliness and neglect. Recently I visited with a bishop who has in his ward more than sixty widows. He beamed, "I love them all!" At least once a week he and his counselors visit them, in addition to the calls made by their home teachers. "They are the joys of our lives," he repeated. He might have said, "Don't you think that is more than our share?"

Another worthy practice in pure religion is a daily telephone call to each housebound person in a neighborhood. A loving, older, widowed lady said, "If I telephone each day, it gives them a lift, and if they don't answer the phone, it lets me know they probably need a personal visit from me." One of these friends could not afford a telephone, so this same sister had a phone installed and took care of the monthly bill.

Pure religion encompasses patience and long-suffering. A father recovering from the wounds of alcoholism has often said, "I am making my way back because my family would not give up on me. Everyone had written me off except my wife and children." How sweet are those words: " I am making my way back because my family would not give up on me."

Pure religion is practiced when we lift the unfortunate and unusual children. Some of God's choicest earthly spirits are those without meaningful parental care. Many are given family relationships by foster parents on a part- or full-time basis.

Pure religion is having the courage to do what is right and let the consequence follow. It is doing the right things for right reasons. To be righteous or serving or loving or obedient to God's laws just to earn praise or recognition is not pure religion. It is being able to withstand ridicule and even temporary unpopularity with some peer groups when you know who you are and for what goals you are reaching. So many of our young people, and older ones also, have developed just such inner strength. They have a great influence for good on others with whom they associate.

Loving those around us includes being sensitive to feelings of others. As is often done, a conducting officer announced that when the deacons were through passing the sacrament, they were invited to go and sit with their families. One father noticed a boy walk out and sit in the foyer. The next week he invited that deacon to sit with his family rather than go through the embarrassment and loneliness caused by not having his own family in attendance. This parent responded to the need of the boy rather than criticizing the leaders for the policy. The actions of this father can be enlarged on and put into practice by every member.

The safety and protection of each person, especially children, should be a concern for all of us. We can be instrumental in assisting in the protection of each other by being aware of potential dangers and being willing to do our part to thwart those who would injure, steal from, or abuse any person, young or old.

Another example of pure religion can be practiced in today s political election processes by those who explain and debate the issues and avoid pettiness and slander. Real political winners are those who would accept defeat rather than participate in character assassination.

Examples of pure religion can be found on every hand. At a funeral about a month ago, I learned of a valiant young lady on a mission in a distant land who, after much prayer and many tears, wrote to her dying mother just before the terminal illness took its toll, and told her that even though she would like to be at her bedside, she would follow her mother's teachings and stay in the mission field to finish her assignment and search out those who wanted to hear the gospel.

From the simple scripture that defines pure religion come great guidelines. To be unspotted from the world, one must avoid all of Satan's evil plans for the inhabitants of the world. Retaliation, fault-finding, deceit, pettiness, hypocrisy, judging, and destroying one another do not belong in the definition of pure religion.

Empathy is sincere love for self and our fellow beings. Henry David Thoreau said, "Could a greater miracle take place than for us to look through each other's eyes for an instant?" If this were possible, I'm sure we could visit and help the widowed and fatherless and all who need our help with the pure love of Christ and thus be responsive to the needs of those around us.

May God help us to learn and live the principles of pure religion. The business of lifting each other is a full-time occupation. Pure religion can never be taught or lived by those who are petty, prejudiced, contentious, or unresponsive to the needs of others. Pure religion is following the teachings of our Savior.

3
"If Thou Endure It Well"

"My son, peace be unto thy soul; thine adversity
and thine afflictions shall be but a small moment;
and then, if thou endure it well, God shall exalt
thee on high; thou shalt triumph over all thy
foes."

(D&C 121:7-8.)

When tragedy, disappointment, and heartache
surface in our lives, it is not unusual for many
of us to become self-condemning and resentful.
In the stress of the situation, we declare, "What have we
done to deserve this? Why does the Lord allow this to
happen to us?"

With heavy hearts and broken spirits the parents of a
wayward child were recently heard to say, "Where did we
go wrong? What have we done to displease the Lord? What
is the Lord trying to tell us? Is this the reward for trying
to be good parents? Why us?"

These were among a flood of questions that came as
they agonized over the serious misconduct of their child.
Their comments and attitude reflected a frightening blend
of resentment, frustration, and self-condemnation.

It was evident that this distraught couple was not to

be calmed or reassured by scriptures or personal observations. Because the child had transgressed, they were
adamant in their feelings that God was displeased with
them. Their attitude reflected bitterness and loss of self-
respect. Momentarily they were letting themselves be con-
sumed and destroyed by the trying circumstances.

In their present tragedy they were not seeking counsel
or comfort; rather, it appeared, they were looking for someone who would suffer with them and join in the chorus
of "If there is a merciful God, why does He allow this to
happen?" We must remember that all suffering is not punishment. It is imperative that we do not allow ourselves
to be destroyed by the conduct of others.

Sometimes we spend so much time trying to determine
what we did wrong in the past to deserve the unpleasant
happenings of the moment that we fail to resolve the challenges of the present. Og Mandino wrote in his book *The
Greatest Miracle in the World,* "If we lock ourselves in a
prison of failure and self-pity, we are the only jailers
. . . we have the only key to our freedom." (New York:
Frederick Fell Publishers, 1975, p. 61.)

We can let ourselves out of such a prison by turning
to the Lord for strength. With His help we can use our
trials as stepping-stones. The keys are in our hands.

"I, the Lord, am bound when ye do what I say; but
when ye do not what I say, ye have no promise." (D&C
82:10.)

If we are offended and resentful, can we believe that
He is bound to help us in our tragedies and disappointments? This scripture does not tell us how or when this
commitment will be effective or realized, but His promise
is real and binding. Our challenge is to endure. There will
always be testings and trials along life's paths. Heartaches
and tragedies need not defeat us if we remember God's
promise.

A worthwhile attitude for all of us could well be, "Help
us, O Lord, to remember thy love for us and help us to

be fortified by Thy strength when our eyes are blurred with tears of sorrow and our vision is limited."

It is expedient for all of us, particularly those who may be weighed down by grief because of acts of misconduct or misfortune, to recall that even the Prophet Joseph Smith had hours of despair because of his very trying experiences in the Liberty Jail. Perhaps he too was entitled to question, "What did I do wrong? What have I done to displease Thee, O Lord? Where have I failed? Why are the answers to my prayers and pleas withheld?" In response to the feelings of his heart and mind he cried out:

"O God, where art thou? And where is the pavilion that covereth thy hiding place?" (D&C 121:1.)

The reassuring response came:

"My son, peace be unto thy soul; thine adversity and thine afflictions shall be but a small moment;

"And then, if thou endure it well, God shall exalt thee on high; thou shalt triumph over all thy foes." (D&C 121:7-8.)

The promise God gave to Joseph Smith is a promise for all of us: "If thou endure it well, God shall exalt thee on high; thou shalt triumph over all thy foes," and also over heartaches caused by misconduct of loved ones.

As we are called upon to suffer we need to ask ourselves the question:

"The Son of Man hath descended below them all. Art thou greater than he?" (D&C 122:8.)

When I think of the Savior's admonition to do cheerfully all things that lie in our power, I think of the father of the prodigal son. The father was heartbroken by the loss and conduct of his wayward son. Yet we have no mention of his lamenting, "Where did I go wrong?" "What have I done to deserve this?" Or, "Where did I fail?"

Instead he seemed to have endured without bitterness his son's misconduct and welcomed him back with love. "For this my son was dead, and is alive again; he was lost, and is found. And they began to be merry." (Luke 15:24.)

When family members disappoint us, we especially need to learn endurance. As long as we exercise love, patience, and understanding, even when no progress is apparent, we are not failing. We must keep trying.

As we viewed on television some of the Olympic games held in Los Angeles, we thrilled at the abilities of these fine young athletes from all over the world. One might easily compare these races and contests of the Olympics with the great race in which we are all involved — the race for eternal life. One gold-medal winner said his success was achieved by being able to endure the pain of commitment and self-discipline.

The Apostle Paul likened life to a great race when he declared: "Know ye not that they which run in a race run all, but one receiveth the prize? So run that ye may obtain." (1 Corinthians 9:24.)

And before the words of Paul fell upon the ears of his listeners, the counsel of the Preacher, the son of David, cautioned: "The race is not to the swift, nor the battle to the strong, but he that endureth to the end shall be saved." (See Ecclesiastes 9:11; Matthew 10:22; Mark 13:13.)

What does it take to endure in the race for eternal life, to become a champion?

To become a winner in the race for eternal life requires effort — constant work, striving, and enduring well with God's help. But the key is that we must take it just one step at a time.

The ingredient that is essential in learning to endure is consistent effort. In our race for eternal life, pain and obstacles will confront all of us. We may experience heartaches, sorrow, death, sins, weakness, disasters, physical illness, pain, mental anguish, unjust criticism, loneliness, or rejection. How we handle these challenges determines whether they become stumbling stones or building blocks. To the valiant these challenges make progress and development possible.

I am acquainted with a young woman who has just

moved here from the eastern part of the United States after
having gone through a painful divorce. She is in the process
of looking for a job. One day an interviewer asked her
what her goals were—where did she think she would be
five years from now? She said to him, "I can't think that
far ahead. For right now I have to just take it one day at
a time." This is what we must do when faced with trials
and setbacks in our lives. Enduring well is accomplished
by personal discipline hour by hour and day by day, not
by public declaration.

There are many types of disappointments and sorrows
with which we may be faced. We have already discussed
the pain of sin in our lives and in the lives of our family
members. Let me share with you other types of happenings
that we may be called upon to endure.

Let me take a few minutes to tell you about a beautiful
young lady of whom we are all very proud. I will identify
her as Diane because that is her real name. Diane was
captain of the University of Utah's first national women's
championship gymnastics team. In Miami, Florida, for the
first-ever American professional tour, she over-rotated on
a practice vault, landed on her neck, and damaged her
spinal cord. Her slender, delicate body, which had endured
hundreds of hours of demanding routines and the accom-
panying torturous training, was broken. The gal with the
dazzling smile who was recognized as the heart of the
team was now faced with the challenge of accepting sym-
pathy as her reward or getting on with her life.

Early in her gymnastics career when someone asked
her, "Aren't you afraid of getting hurt?" she replied, "No,
you take the glory and you take the knocks. I'll just take
whatever comes."

Diane's capacity to cope and get on with her life is best
measured by her graduating from college two and one-
half years after being paralyzed from the chest down.
Wheelchair-bound, she seldom missed a class, was a good
student, and was popular with classmates and instructors.

Just a few weeks ago Diane wheeled herself into a third-grade classroom in a Salt Lake area elementary school, swallowed hard, and faced the curious students as their nervous teacher. "I've always wanted to be a teacher," she says with conviction. "I can't think of anything I'd want to do more." "How about performing in the Olympics?" she was asked. "Yes," she responds wistfully, "I wanted that a lot, too."

How refreshing is her enduring attitude: "I always got around fairly well on campus in my wheelchair alone, but when I came to steep hills I made friends in a hurry."

Diane has taken the knocks and the glory. She cares and she shares. She finds fun where others may not see it: "I'm genuinely happy and content with my life. I'm not bitter or angry. In a way I'm just as athletic as I ever was."

With her superb attitude and self-discipline, and with the help of a loving family, friends, and students, she continues to "go for the gold." Diane, thank you for teaching us what enduring is all about.

In whatever circumstance we may find ourselves, whether in the midst of tragedy, the pain of misconduct, or merely the daily struggle to live the life of a faithful Latter-day Saint, we must remember "the race is not to the swift, nor the battle to the strong, but he that endureth to the end shall be saved."

Sometimes as children we were told everything would be all right. But life is not like that. No matter who you are, you will have problems. Tragedy and frustration are the unexpected intruders on life's plans. Someone has said, "Life is what happens to you while you are making other plans." It is important that we not look upon our afflictions as a punishment from God. True, our own actions may cause some of our problems, but often there is no evident misconduct that has caused our trials. Just the normal journey through life teaches us that nothing worthwhile comes easy.

Sometimes the most challenging form of endurance is found in trying to stay with our priorities, commitments, and assignments. How easy it is for some of us to lose our way when the unexpected, and seemingly undeserved, surface in our lives. Greatness is best measured by how well an individual responds to the happenings in life that appear to be totally unfair, unreasonable, and undeserved. Sometimes we are inclined to put up with a situation rather than endure. To endure is to bear up under, to stand firm against, to suffer without yielding, to continue to be, or to exhibit the state or power of lasting.

Day by day we can make the effort to gain the power to last and to suffer without yielding. Inspiration and motivation are found in many places—from the cases I have cited and from many other examples to be seen on every hand. We can also receive strength from studying the scriptures and praying constantly.

Friends and loved ones often offer strength and support when our own resolve is weak. In turn, our own strength and capacity will be doubled when we help others endure.

I pray that God will help us to endure well, with purpose and power. When we so do, the meaningful declaration in 2 Timothy 4:7 will take on a new dimension:

"I have fought a good fight, I have finished my course, I have kept the faith."

When heartaches, tragedies, disappointments, injury, unusual attention, fame, or excessive prosperity become part of our lives, our challenges and responsibilities will be to endure them well. God will assist us in our quest to conquer, triumph, and continue if we humbly rededicate ourselves to the meaningful declaration "We have endured many things, and hope to be able to endure all things." (Articles of Faith 1:13.)

God does live. Jesus is the Christ. One of His marks of greatness, His endurance, stands as a constant beacon for us to emulate. During His earthly sojourn He endured well as He suffered agony and rejection in their deepest forms. I bear my witness that God will help us to endure as we put forth the effort to live His teachings, seek His guidance, and keep His commandments.

4
Choose the Good Part

"A good man out of the good treasure of the
heart bringeth forth good things."
(Matthew 12:35.)

A few weeks ago while in Idaho reorganizing a stake
presidency, I not only met some outstanding
priesthood leaders and set three of them apart as
a new stake presidency, but I also met a very special young
lady I will not soon forget. The newly called presidency,
one of whom was serving as a bishop at the time, asked
if I could interview a prospective bishop so if he were
cleared he could be installed the following Sunday after
conference. The appointment was made. I sat in a private
office with a well-groomed, attractive couple.

After a few words of greeting and introductions, I
looked at her and said, "Tell me about your husband."
She hesitated and finally said, "Elder Ashton, I really don't
know him very well." Since this was a most unusual response, I promptly said, "Please tell me about that." She
responded with, "We have only been married three
weeks."

This young couple, both in their early thirties, he an
attorney and she a schoolteacher, were still honeymoon-

ing, and their deep, newly found love for each other was most evident. When I said, "I want to talk to the two of you about your husband becoming a bishop," she said, "Some nights ago I had a dream indicating Randy would be a bishop. I just hoped it wouldn't come too soon." She continued with, "Even though we are newlyweds [and incidentally, they told me the reason they had waited until their thirties to marry was because they had spent a long time finding each other], if you are impressed to call Randy to be a bishop, he will be a good one, and I will help him."

What a beautiful attitude. What sustaining support. Her commitment to her husband, Church, and self was made long before I asked my questions. She had resolved to choose the good part, reminding me of the meaningful statement made about Mary in Luke 10:42: "One thing is needful: and Mary hath chosen that good part, which shall not be taken away from her."

The more I become involved in the Church and in communities worldwide, the greater becomes my appreciation and respect for good women. I would like to pay sincere tribute and give encouragement to these special ladies. My personal definition of a good woman is any woman who is moving in the right direction. I humbly thank God constantly for their courage, strength, and commitment. Through you noble sisters, each in different circumstances in life, by your example, encouragement, conduct, and personal integrity, God's work goes forward with greater purpose and accomplishment.

Let me share with you some recent experiences, correspondence, and observations, particularly with the single women in the Church. Most of them are doing well in the situations in which they find themselves. They, however, sincerely need our love, encouragement, and respect. They, along with all of the rest of us, need not be resigned to their present status or role. Eternal progression is a basic part of the gospel of Jesus Christ. Happiness, enthusiasm, and joy in daily living are mandatory if we would move forward and choose the good part.

The principles of the gospel of Jesus Christ will never change, but environment, circumstances, institutions, and cultural patterns do. Our challenge is to move forward in our present realms with commitment and enthusiasm. We must do our part to progress and enjoy life while we are in the process of meeting our situations.

The mother of a Filipino missionary recently wrote to her son's mission president: "Thank you so much for the spiritual support and counsel that you give to my son. . . . Being a lone parent for almost eight years would have been very hard for me, were it not for the gospel's truthfulness. I know God lives and He loves me. He hears and answers my earnest and sincere prayers. I still have seven children, including our missionary, under my care. The Lord has blessed me with a talent that has helped me through the years to support my family. I earn a living by serving as a dressmaker. I'm indeed grateful for my 'Church family'—members who have inspired me and helped me to accept cheerfully and confidently my single parenthood."

Here is a sister who has learned that God is well pleased with families of one or more if they include Him and adhere to His teachings.

Oh, how powerful are good women who choose the good part.

And although He will always be at our side if we will but invite Him, never will He take from His children the great gift of agency—the power to choose. Young mothers (single or otherwise) must learn to use this power wisely. There may be times when more than one course of action is placed before us. Each is right. It is then that wise and prudent decisions must be made, taking into consideration the season of life and the pertinent facts.

Some mothers seem to have the capacity and energy to make their children's clothes, bake, give piano lessons, go to Relief Society, teach Sunday School, attend parent-teacher association meetings, and so on. Other mothers look upon such women as models and feel inadequate, depressed, and think they are failures when they make comparisons.

We should not allow ourselves to be trapped into such damaging inferiority feelings. This is another tool of Satan. Many seem to put too much pressure on themselves to be a "supermom" or "superwoman."

Sisters, do not allow yourselves to be made to feel inadequate or frustrated because you cannot do everything others seem to be accomplishing. Rather, each should assess her own situation, her own energy, and her own talents, and then choose the best way to mold her family into a team, a unit that works together and supports each other. Only you and your Father in Heaven know your needs, strengths, and desires. Around this knowledge your personal course must be charted and your choices made.

Let me share another example of a courageous single mother who has chosen the good part and effectively lives within her situation. She is in her mid-thirties and has suffered much heartache in her life. Shortly after she and her husband were married in the temple, he became inactive. This man chose to spend most of his time with male companions. There was no concern for the welfare of his family nor any desire to build a meaningful relationship with his wife. Church activities became nonexistent in his life, and soon he was led down the path of transgression.

Of necessity this lovely woman is providing financially for herself and her children. Her paramount goal is to make a happy home environment in which her boys and girls can feel emotional, financial, and spiritual security. For ten years their home was deprived of these ingredients of happiness.

Even though she hopes that marriage may come again sometime in the future, for the present she is concerned with the needs of her children and is working to build a strong family unit centered around the Church and its teachings.

As a single parent she has chosen the good part.

In times of hurt and discouragement, it may be consoling for her and for all of us to recall that no one can do anything permanently to us that will last for eternity. Only we ourselves can affect our eternal progression.

There is a temptation on the part of some of our sisters who have never married to give up, to stop trying, to think of what they don't have in life instead of what they do have. It is important for them to never give up, to never cease living. As Sister Carol Clark has so beautifully stated: "The personal challenge is not to wait successfully but to live richly, fully, joyfully. The goal is not to wait for the right person but to *be* the right person." (*A Singular Life: Perspectives for the Single Woman* [Salt Lake City: Deseret Book Co., 1974], p. 9.) May I emphasize the word *live*. Live richly, fully, joyfully. Be excited about your chance to grow and develop your potential. Be excited about life and the opportunities and privileges that the Lord has given you.

Make a decision as to the kind of person you want to be regardless of external circumstances. The first challenge in life is to learn, accept, and internalize "Who am I?" If this question is researched carefully in the scriptures and in Church teachings, the importance of each and every soul will be verified. A good self-image is one of the most important and necessary steps in facing life. So often we believe about ourselves only the things that others have implanted. There is no woman in or out of the Church who is not a loved child of God—not one!

In Psalms 8:4-5 we read: "What is man, that thou art mindful of him? and the son of man, that thou visitest him? For thou hast made him a little lower than the angels, and hast crowned him with glory and honour."

But Satan is ever present, trying to destroy our glory and remove our crown. One of his most powerful tools is discouragement. Single sisters, don't let your discouragement make Satan rejoice.

Sometimes singles are inclined to become wrapped up

in themselves rather than searching for a way to affect the future. Become success oriented. Know that you can succeed. Believe that you can succeed. Step into auxiliary organizations of the Church and into community organizations and make your presence felt.

Thinking and acting women today are taking part in making history in one of the greatest periods of humanity. Their personal contributions not only make the difference today, but their good works have mighty import upon the future. As circles of activity widen, so will the number of friends and acquaintances widen. And then the influence of good women will have an even greater impact on those with whom they associate.

We must constantly remember it is not our situation or problems that make us unhappy; it is our failure to properly resolve them.

Someone has said, "Happiness is like a butterfly. The more you chase it, the more it will elude you. But if you turn your attention to other things, it comes and sits softly on your shoulder." (Nathaniel Hawthorne, quoted in *Reader's Digest*, April 1982, p. 148.)

In the Church our leaders have a great desire and spend much thought and prayer in trying to offer guidelines that may help with solutions. In reference to a recent letter in which the First Presidency gave guidelines for membership in singles wards, let me emphasize it is contemplated that no abrupt changes in existing programs be made without considering their impact on the lives of those who are presently involved in singles wards. Stake presidents are now authorized to make exceptions to the general policy after consultation and joint agreement with the bishop involved.

No one should be asked to leave. While there are definite advantages, with other things being equal, to an older single person being active in his or her own conventional ward, no one should be displaced or left to feel unwanted when proper marriage opportunities fail to develop. Certain age restrictions are prescribed by policy guidelines for good reasons, but no one should feel displaced or terminated, if you please, through abrupt changes.

Programs are planned and implemented with love and concern for each person in the Church. The desire is to offer opportunities for growth, development, and happiness for all members. With each passing year, the value of our sisters who are living without companions becomes more apparent. Strong leaders, good teachers, and dedicated mothers constantly emerge from this group of sisters. They live and serve with courage and ingenuity. Through perseverance they are finding success.

To be in control of your life, to be a success regardless of your situation, whether happily married, unhappily married, a single parent, a widow, or a wife of an inactive husband, I recommend that you come to know your Father in heaven. Come to love Him, and always remember that He loves you and will give you guidance and support if you will but give Him the chance. Include Him in your decision making. Include Him when you take inventory of your personal worth. "For behold, this life is the time for men [and women] to prepare to meet God; yea, behold the day of this life is the day for men [and women] to perform their labors." (Alma 34:32.)

Set your goals—without goals you can't measure your progress. But don't become frustrated because there are no obvious victories. Remind yourself that striving can be more important than arriving. If you are striving for excellence—if you are trying your best day by day with the wisest use of your time and energy to reach realistic goals—you are a success.

Commune daily with your Heavenly Father, who knows you best of all. He knows your talents, your strengths, and your weaknesses. You are here on the earth at this time to develop and refine these characteristics. I promise you He will help you. He is aware of your needs. He is aware of your unanswered prayers.

God bless our valiant women members. You are choice in His and our eyes. We pray that with His help and our personal efforts happiness will be achieved. Certainly when we choose the good part, regardless of our current circumstances or situations, life will be lived to the fullest.

5
Carry Your Cross

"If any man will come after me, let him deny
himself, and take up his cross, and follow me."
(Matthew 16:24.)

W hy don't you have crosses on your buildings of
worship?" "Why aren't your chapels built in
the shape of a cross?" "Why don't you encourage your people to wear and display crosses?" "What
is the Church's policy toward crosses?"

From Matthew 16:24-25: "Then said Jesus unto his disciples, If any man will come after me, let him deny himself,
and take up his cross, and follow me. For whosoever will
save his life shall lose it: and whosoever will lose his life
for my sake shall find it."

We in The Church of Jesus Christ of Latter-day Saints,
in response to these questions, try to teach our people to
carry their crosses rather than display or wear them. Over
the centuries the cross has been recognized as a symbol
of Christianity in the minds of millions. The Savior Himself
has given us the bread and water as emblems of His sacrifice and death.

My message to you this day is to take up your cross.
Take yourself the way you are and lift yourself in the

31

direction of the better. Regardless of where you have been, what you have done, or what you haven't done, trust God, believe on Him, relate to Him, worship Him as you carry your cross with dignity and determination.

We save our lives by losing them for His sake. As you find yourself, you will find God. This is true. I declare that to you. It is His promise. Take up the real cross of Jesus Christ.

What kind of cross do you bear? What is its shape, weight, size, or dimension? We all have them. Some are very visible, while others are not always evident. Sometimes the heaviest personal cross could be to carry no cross at all. Some crosses we bear are these (maybe you will relate to one or more): the cross of loneliness; the cross of physical limitations — the loss of a leg, an arm, hearing, seeing, mobility — obvious crosses (we see people with these crosses and admire their strength in carrying them with dignity); the cross of poor health; the cross of transgression; the cross of success; the cross of temptation; the cross of beauty, fame, or wealth; the cross of financial burdens; the cross of criticism; the cross of peer rejection.

What if we are challenged with more than one cross? A beautiful young lady once said to me, "Elder Ashton, it just isn't time for me to have another cross. I'm not quite used to the one I'm carrying now. How can I handle both?" Truly, suffering is part of our mortal existence, and suffering is not all bad.

Today I'd like to talk in more detail about certain crosses in life that are real, but that are not always recognized or visible. Number 1 is the cross of the violated trust — on the part of a parent, a family member, a teacher, a bishop, a stake presidency member, a boyfriend, a classmate, a returned missionary, a girlfriend, and so on. Some of us let an act of mistrust on the part of someone close to us shatter our todays and tomorrows. A friend of mine said, "When my endowed father left Mom for a scheming secretary, it was more than I could bear." She was bitter. This cross was causing her to crumble. She had never looked upon it as a cross, but it was a cross of hatred and resentment: "I can't believe my father would let us down! What is the use?"

Another one: "When my boyfriend talked me into a couple of drinks and then took advantage of me morally, it caused me to never trust anyone again." This cross is breaking her because she has not decided that with God's help she can carry it. Another one I heard from a broken-hearted wife of a year and a half: "My husband, a returned missionary, told me it was okay, so I did it" — compromising immoral intimacies.

And I received this in a letter from the father of two BYU coeds who were the victims of improper conduct on the part of imperfect people on campus — the father and mother were shattered: "We can't stand to believe and know that that could happen to our students at Brigham Young University!"

We're proud of BYU, but it is made up of imperfect people, and sometimes very imperfect things happen there even though we thank God that they are fewer there than at any other university we know of.

Can even these hidden crosses be carried for future strength instead of causing us to fall and not get back up? "Behold, he who has repented of his sins, the same is forgiven, and I, the Lord, remember them no more." (D&C 58:42.) Sometimes it is easier for the Lord not to remember our sins than it is for us. They become a cross because we will not do ourselves the favor of carrying on. "By this ye may know if a man repenteth of his sins — behold, he will confess them and forsake them." (D&C 58:43.) Can you carry appropriately the cross of forgiveness? Some of us would rather carry a cross than confess and start anew.

George Q. Cannon, in his wonderful book *The Life of Joseph Smith the Prophet*, points out repeatedly that the greatest cross that Joseph Smith had to bear — and he had many — was the cross of trusted friends who were not worthy of the word *trust*. His heartaches, his death, his inconveniences were caused by those in whom his trust had been misplaced.

Number 2, another cross that isn't always visible but on occasion can be very heavy and worrisome, is the cross of self-unacceptance—a continuing willingness to reject oneself through self-condemnation and low self-appraisal. Can you find it in your heart to once in a while give yourself a good grade on your behavior? Or do you give yourself low marks no matter what you do because you carry the cross of self-unacceptance?

An unannounced, but obviously self-imposed, personal-enemy-number-1 status in regard to ourselves is a heavy cross. Sometimes in solitude and in humility there is only one person on earth that can be your advocate, and that must be you—someone who will not condemn you under that cross and cause you to fail.

Being down on ourselves is destructive. As we bear this kind of a cross we have a tendency to reach only the low levels we expect of ourselves. What a cross it is to convince yourself, "I'm no good. I can't do it. I can't make it." What a cross! It doesn't even show. But by lifting that cross we can become more than we would have been had we not been required to carry the cross. Some of us spend too much time protecting our wounded selves.

Always wishing you were some other person with greater talents and greater strengths is a handicap—it's a cross that is not visible, but it is so real. Is it a cross to bear when we realize that with God's help we can overcome, we can be victorious, and we can accomplish much?

I love the following quotation. I suppose I use it more than any other one when I try to give encouragement to family and friends like you: "When Ammon had said these words, his brother Aaron rebuked him, saying: Ammon, I fear that thy joy doth carry thee away unto boasting.

"But Ammon said unto him: I do not boast in my own strength, nor in my own wisdom; but behold, my joy is full, yea, my heart is brim with joy, and I will rejoice in my God. Yea, I know that I am nothing; as to my strength I am weak; therefore I will not boast of myself, but I will boast of my God, for in his strength I can do all things." (Alma 26:10-12.)

I wish we believed that. I wish we practiced that. I wish we knew that. There are days when people who have been called to positions of responsibility, as I have been, have to humbly say, "God, I'm weak, but with your help I can do it," and give Him a chance to help lift that cross of inadequate strength.

"Yea, behold, many mighty miracles we have wrought in this land, for which we will praise his name forever. Behold, how many thousands of our brethren has he loosed from the pains of hell; and they are brought to sing redeeming love, and this because of the power of his word which is in us, therefore have we not great reason to rejoice?"(Alma 26:12-13.)

It is a fact of life that God can make our crosses easier to bear if we are but willing to admit that we have them and then seek His help. In D&C 56:2 we read: "He that will not take up his cross and follow me, and keep my commandments, the same shall not be saved."

A willingness to take yourself as you are and build from there is pleasing to God. If you have more than one cross — three or four — maybe you could build a ladder out of them and use them to climb to new heights. Sometimes becoming is more important than achieving or arriving. I'm not talking about self-indulgence. I'm talking about self-acceptance. All tomorrows can be in our favor if we carry on in a spirit of commitment and self-encouragement.

Number 3 is the cross of resisting counsel. Some of us have a tendency to resent, resist, rebel, and delay, and to debate worthy direction, supervision, and communication. I plead with you to avoid the ranks of professional counsel resisters, who make such statements as, "Who are you to tell me?" "I didn't come here to be babysat." "Why all the restrictions?" "Where does free agency come in?" "Why don't you just leave me alone?" Some carry that heavy cross of wanting to rebel or to resist counsel from friends. They reject that counsel because it may cause inconvenience, or because they may not be able to see far enough ahead to see its value.

In D&C 23:6, Joseph Knight was counseled to pray: "Behold, I manifest unto you, Joseph Knight, by these words, that you must take up your cross, in the which you must pray vocally before the world as well as in secret, and in your family, and among your friends, and in all places." Sometimes we are given crosses so we can be taught to pray. Crosses become lighter and more manageable when we learn to pray and when we learn to patiently wait for the answers to our prayers.

An unwillingness to listen and learn can be a silent cross of considerable weight. Carry the cross of constant prayer even when answers are slow in coming or difficult to accept.

Number 4 is the cross of living among many Mormons. Did you ever think of it as a cross? Having many Mormons for many Church assignments may not be as rewarding and developing as situations in which there are few Mormons to do many Church responsibilities. You may come from a location where your strength, commitment, and attendance made the difference. Sometimes it's easy to let the cross of many Mormons make us weak because we feel in our hearts that someone else will do what needs to be done. Complacency, lack of enthusiasm and involvement, can be the fruit of having too many of us together. Often there is great strength and development where Mormons are in the minority. It's like being the deacon (one of two in a small branch) who said, "I must be awfully important because I'm 50 percent."

How sad, and I hope untrue, is the statement, "There aren't enough Church jobs to go around." Beware of the cross of complacency and an attitude of not being needed.

It is a cross when you say, "Someone else can do that. I'll wait for another assignment."

Number 5 is the cross of caustic comments — to take pleasure in constantly putting people down, in murmuring, ridicule, contention, slander, gossip; in putting yourself down and enjoying it. Avoid being a rumor reservoir. If you're part of a rumor reservoir, you're entitled to drown. Some people enjoy being caustic. Some have careless and sharp tongues as crosses. Our job is not to live with them, but to reshape and manage our own tongue and mind if we enjoy being caustic.

A home of contention is more than a cross, it is a curse. Some homes without decoration and rehearsal train the inhabitants to be critical. This is an invisible cross of tremendous power, and it is destructive if we carry it. From 2 Nephi 26:32: "The Lord God hath commanded that men should not . . . contend one with another." A caustic tongue can construct additional crosses that are so unnecessary. A critical tongue is a cross easily removed, but only you can do it.

Cross number 6 is the cross of adulation. Be careful, be aware, be wise when people speak well of you. When people treat you with great respect and love, be careful, be aware, be wise. When you are honored, pointed out, and recognized, it can be a cross, especially if you believe what is said about you. Being a BYU student, a Mormon, a returned missionary, a member of the BYU faculty or administration, a General Authority, a Prophet, temple-married — some people know these identifications for you and, although you might take them for granted, they're lofty. But these can be crosses, and you must bear them well.

Praise of the world can be a heavy cross. How often I have heard it said over the years, "He was great until he became successful, and then he couldn't handle it." I'm not talking about money and position. I'm talking about recognition, even in Church responsibilities. We should

honor callings and responsibilities and realize that what
we are and what we do will depend on the strength of the
cross.

I would pray that we would avoid being carried away
by praise, success, or even achieving goals that we have
set for ourselves. In Mormon 8:38-39 we read: "O ye pol-
lutions, ye hypocrites, ye teachers, who sell yourselves for
that which will canker, why have ye polluted the holy
church of God? Why are ye ashamed to take upon you the
name of Christ? Why do ye not think that greater is the
value of an endless happiness than that misery which never
dies—because of the praise of the world? Why do ye adorn
yourselves with that which hath no life, and yet suffer the
hungry, and the needy, and the naked, and the sick and
the afflicted to pass by you, and notice them not?"

How great, how strong, how pleasing it is to be recognized, honored, and respected, but we must realize in
our hearts that true greatness is visiting with the Savior
Jesus Christ by helping those who are sick, afflicted, discouraged, homeless, and burdened with crosses.

In conclusion, we do not reverence crosses. As stated
in the beginning, ours is to carry them with dignity and
power. Our right and responsibility is to carry our crosses,
and while we are doing so to have the good sense and
judgment to count our blessings. These phrases you'll recognize:

> When upon life's billows you are tempest-tossed,
> When you are discouraged, thinking all is lost,
> Count your many blessings; name them one by one,
> And it will surprise you what the Lord has done.
> Count your blessings; name them one by one.
> Count your blessings; see what God hath done.
> Count your blessings; name them one by one
> [as you carry your cross].
> Count your many blessings; see what God hath done.
>
> Are you ever burdened with a load of care?
> Does the cross seem heavy you are called to bear?

Count your many blessings; every doubt will fly,
And you will be singing as the days go by.
Count your blessings; name them one by one.
Count your blessings; see what God hath done.
Count your blessings; name them one by one.
Count your many blessings; see what God hath done.
(Hymns, no. 241.)

There is an aid, there is a strength, there is a power when we count our blessings as we labor under crosses that sometimes seem unreasonable and unfair but that can be for our good and for our strength. I bear special witness to you that carrying our crosses and following our Lord will bring strength, peace, and purpose in our quest for the abundant life. God has made this promise. Carry your crosses with strength, with purpose, and while you do, count the blessings of God's strength.

6
Quiet Giving

"Take heed that ye do not your alms before men
to be seen of them; . . . that thine alms may be
in secret; and thy Father who seeth in secret,
himself shall reward thee openly."
(3 Nephi 13:1, 4.)

Some weeks ago a university president shared with me his pleasure in receiving a substantial monetary contribution from an unexpected donor. The giver said she wanted the money to go to her state institution of higher learning but insisted no one be told of her gift. When asked why, she said, "I have come to know the personal benefits of quiet giving."

To me it is heartwarming to hear of such people. Incidentally, while she is still unknown to me because the president maintains his pledge, I salute her and others who find satisfaction in realizing giving is its own reward.

Is this quiet giving a new way of life? A new source of satisfaction? Let me answer these questions by sharing the following.

"When he was come down from the mountain, great multitudes followed him. And, behold, there came a leper and worshipped him, saying, Lord, if thou wilt, thou canst make me clean. And Jesus put forth his hand, and touched him, saying, I will; be thou clean. And immediately his leprosy was cleansed. And Jesus saith unto him, *See thou tell no man;* but go thy way, shew thyself to the priest, and offer the gift that Moses commanded, for a testimony unto them." (Matthew 8:1-4; italics added.)

"And when Jesus departed thence, two blind men followed him, crying, and saying, Thou Son of David, have mercy on us. And when he was come into the house, the blind men came to him: and Jesus saith unto them, Believe ye that I am able to do this? They said unto him, Yea, Lord. Then touched he their eyes, saying, According to your faith be it unto you. And their eyes were opened; and Jesus straitly charged them, saying, *See that no man know it.* But they, when they were departed, spread abroad his fame in all that country." (Matthew 9:27-31; italics added.)

Jesus Christ, the mortal Messiah, pointed the way. His life encompassed quiet giving.

Much has been written and spoken over the years about the virtues of the cheerful giver. I would like to pay special tribute to quiet givers and recommend to others the joy and satisfaction that can come from quiet sharing. The Savior in His powerful and loving sermon to the Nephites in 3 Nephi, chapter 13, points the way for daily and eternal rewards as we conform.

"Verily, verily, I say that I would that ye should do alms unto the poor; but take heed that ye do not your alms before men to be seen of them; otherwise you have no reward of your Father who is in heaven. Therefore, when ye shall do your alms do not sound a trumpet before you, as will hypocrites do in the synagogues and in the streets, that they may have glory of men. Verily I say unto you, they have their reward. But when thou doest alms let not thy left hand know what thy right hand doeth; that thine alms may be in secret; and thy Father who seeth in secret, himself shall reward thee openly." (3 Nephi 13:1-4.)

Alms by definition is a gift or gifts to the poor or needy. A gift is something that is given, goods, money, or time. The Savior lived the quiet giving life. We should do good quietly, privately, and let our deeds be discovered accidentally. God knows. You know. The recipient knows. What else matters? Proper giving and sharing in God's sight will be rewarded openly. Quiet giving puts into action the admonition that we be doers of the word.

I am thinking of an elderly widow who is housebound and lives alone. Every morning she uses her telephone and calls four of her widow associates who are alone. She greets them with, "Are you all right, dear?" She doesn't tell people that this is one of her quiet forms of giving and sharing. She just does it. Those who are the recipients of her call and generosity are the ones who share her Christlike service, and tell people like you and me about it. Should one of her daily calls ever result in no answer, someone would be alerted immediately to find out why. Her quiet giving of time and self in this way could make the difference between life and death, between illness or pain and needed attention. Her friends expect her daily calls and look forward to the caring contact.

I am also thinking of another friend who is a quiet giver. He provides money to be given to needy missionaries somewhere in the world. His only requirement is that it be given to a missionary who is in need. He insists that the receiver not know from whom the money comes. His instructions are: "When these dollars have been given away, let me know and I will replace them so that this deed may be done on a perpetual basis." His joy is found in the giving, not in the recognition.

Sometimes we have a tendency to give with an anticipation of being vocally rewarded by the recipient or other family members. I am thinking of someone who recently sent a missionary a gift in the form of cash, and almost before the recipient would have time to receive it the giver was asking the parents of the missionary if their son had received it.

Quiet giving brings its own lasting reward.

In Luke 11:41 we are instructed, "But rather give alms of such things as ye have."

The Savior teaches us the value of quiet or silent prayers: "When thou prayest thou shalt not do as the hypocrites, for they love to pray, standing in the synagogues and in the corners of the streets, that they may be seen of men. Verily I say unto you, they have their reward. But thou, when thou prayest, enter into thy closet, and when thou hast shut thy door, pray to thy Father who is in secret; and thy Father, who seeth in secret, shall reward thee openly. But when ye pray, use not vain repetitions, as the heathen, for they think that they shall be heard for their much speaking. Be not ye therefore like unto them, for your Father knoweth what things ye have need of before ye ask him." (3 Nephi 13:5-8.)

Perhaps we would do well to involve ourselves in more and more quiet saying of prayers. There are strength, power, and discipline rewards in communicating with God on a continuing personal and private basis. Quietly we can pray for the patience to have our secret prayers answered. Sometimes we fail to recognize answered prayers because we are expecting more than quiet answers.

"After this manner therefore pray ye: Our Father who art in heaven, hallowed be thy name. Thy will be done on earth as it is in heaven. And forgive us our debts, as we forgive our debtors. And lead us not into temptation, but deliver us from evil. For thine is the kingdom, and the power, and the glory, forever. Amen." (3 Nephi 13:9-13.)

In Alma 34:28 we read, "Impart of your substance [prayer], if ye have, to those who stand in need." The Lord's prayer sets the proper pattern for prayers for those who would share and be concerned with not only God but all others. I love its quiet composition and selfless approach.

"But this is not all; ye must pour out your souls in your closets, and your secret places, and in your wilderness.

Yea, and when you do not cry unto the Lord, let your hearts be full, drawn out in prayer unto him continually for your welfare, and also for the welfare of those who are around you." (Alma 34:26-28.) What a joy the quiet giving of ourselves in prayer brings when our primary concern is "those who are around you."

Fasting can also be appropriately accomplished in an attitude and setting of quiet giving. Fasting quietly for the benefit of another is an inner evidence of true love. It brings rewarding peace.

"Moreover, when ye fast be not as the hypocrites, of a sad countenance, for they disfigure their faces that they may appear unto men to fast. Verily I say unto you, they have their reward. That thou appear not unto men to fast, but unto thy Father, who is in secret; and thy Father, who seeth in secret, shall reward thee openly." (3 Nephi 13:16, 18.)

Fasting is best participated in without eternal evidence of suffering, pain, or unnecessary announcements. Not only is fasting a private privilege, but it makes possible unpretentious giving to the needy. Self-discipline and self-denial are also worthy personal fruits of the fast. In quiet humility if food is offered to us during our fast, perhaps "No thank you" is preferable to the announcement, "I am fasting today." Let your fasting come as a blessing to others and yourself rather than as an announced sacrifice.

Quiet giving is more rewarding than personal getting. True growth comes from sharing, not accumulating. Attainment of wealth without sharing is empty.

"Lay not up for yourselves treasures upon earth, where moth and dust doth corrupt, and thieves break through and steal; but lay up for yourselves treasures in heaven, where neither moth nor rust doth corrupt, and where thieves do not break through nor steal. For where your treasure is, there will your heart be also." (3 Nephi 13:19-21.)

Finally there is no greater earthly reward than the quiet

giving of self. Giving of self without desire for recognition is Christ-centered living. Albert Schweitzer said the following: "I do not know where all of you are going or what you will do, but let me tell you simply this: unless you set aside some portion of your lives to help and serve those less fortunate than yourselves, you will really not be happy."

"For I was an hungred, and ye gave me meat: I was thirsty, and ye gave me drink: I was a stranger, and ye took me in: Naked, and ye clothed me: I was sick, and ye visited me: I was in prison, and ye came unto me.

"Then shall the righteous answer him, saying, Lord, when saw we thee an hungred, and fed thee? or thirsty, and gave thee drink? When saw we thee a stranger, and took thee in? or naked, and clothed thee? Or when saw we thee sick, or in prison, and came unto thee? And the King shall answer and say unto them, Verily I say unto you, Inasmuch as ye have done it unto one of the least of these my brethren, ye have done it unto me." (Matthew 25:35-40.)

Peter's gift to the lame man in the name of Jesus Christ of Nazareth at the gates of the temple was quiet giving in its highest form.

"Now Peter and John went up together into the temple at the hour of prayer, being the ninth hour. And a certain man lame from his mother's womb was carried, whom they laid daily at the gate of the temple which is called Beautiful, to ask alms of them that entered into the temple: who seeing Peter and John about to go into the temple asked an alms.

"And Peter, fastening his eyes upon him with John, said, Look on us. And he gave heed unto them, expecting to receive something of them. Then Peter said, Silver and gold have I none; but such as I have give I thee: In the name of Jesus Christ of Nazareth rise up and walk." (Acts 3:1-6.)

The quiet giver looks, listens, hears, and finds ways to help. He needs no recognition.

May we learn from the New Testament, the Book of Mormon, and life's journeys the personal and rewarding benefits of the quiet giving of alms, prayer, fasting, and self.

7
The Word Is Commitment

"Verily I say, men should be anxiously engaged
in a good cause, and do many things of their
own free will, and bring to pass much righteousness."

(D&C 58:27.)

Recently I had the opportunity of congratulating a
special young lady upon her graduation from college. Knowing she had achieved this lofty goal under extreme difficulties, I said, "Would you mind telling
me in one word how you were able to achieve this great
accomplishment?" While she paused momentarily, words
like *courage, determination,* and *faith* flashed through my
mind as I anticipated her answer. Then without hesitation
she said, "Elder Ashton, the word is *commitment.*"

Most of us who have ever heard of the great American
leader Abraham Lincoln will recall what he said of his
mother: "All that I am, all that I hope to be, I owe to my
Angel mother." (In *Abraham Lincoln's Philosophy of Common
Sense,* ed. Edward J. Kempf [New York: The New York
Academy of Sciences, 1965], p. 60.) But how many of us
know what his mother's last words to him were? They
were "Be something, Abe."

Not only is this wise counsel, but it also expresses the yearnings of most fathers' and mothers' hearts to have their children be something. Simple terms, but, oh, how powerful, "Be something." I am so pleased she didn't say, "Be someone." She said, "Be something, Abe." There is a significant difference. In the dictionary *someone* is defined as "conceived or thought of, but not definitely known," while *something* is identified as "a person or thing of importance."

Abraham Lincoln's mother knew her son, his potential, and the rocky roads ahead of him; hence, she wanted him to commit himself promptly to being steadfast and immovable in living and promoting deeds of courage and faith in the lives of all mankind.

A word of hope is poured out on every generation of people by those who advocate accomplishment, an exemplary life, living up to one's abilities, and keeping one's commitments.

True happiness is not made in getting something. True happiness is becoming something. This can be done by being committed to lofty goals. We cannot become something without commitment.

Commitment as a word cannot stand alone. We must always ask, "Committed to what?" As all of us blend into the programs of the Church, it behooves us to set goals for ourselves in order to reap the blessings of self-improvement and excellent performance in given assignments.

"Verily I say, men should be anxiously engaged in a good cause, and do many things of their own free will, and bring to pass much righteousness; for the power is in them, wherein they are agents unto themselves. And inasmuch as men do good they shall in nowise lose their reward. But he that doeth not anything until he is commanded, and receiveth a commandment with doubtful heart, and keepeth it with slothfulness, the same is damned." (D&C 58:27-29.)

As we search for good causes, we must consider our

own needs, but also we must live in compliance with gospel teachings.

President Spencer W. Kimball at the Regional Representatives Seminar of April 3, 1975, said, "I believe in goals, but I believe that the individual should set his own. Goals should always be made to a point that will make us reach and strain. Success should not necessarily be gauged by always reaching the goal set, but by progress and attainment."

In setting our own goals we need to examine our own needs and abilities. The direction in which we are moving is more important than where we are at the moment. Goal-setting should cause us to stretch as we make our way.

Self-examination is most difficult. Surveys have shown that most people take credit for success to themselves, but blame their failures on external forces or other people. It would be well, when confronted with problems, to be able to ask the same questions the Twelve Apostles asked during the Last Supper.

"Now when the even was come, he sat down with the twelve. And as they did eat, he said, Verily I say unto you, that one of you shall betray me. And they were exceeding sorrowful, and began every one of them to say unto him, Lord, is it I?" (Matthew 26:20-22.)

When our progress seems to be at a standstill, it is well for us to ask who is at fault. Is it I? Am I sufficiently committed to righteous goals? Do I have the courage, fortitude, and wisdom to apply self-examination — or will I be inclined to try to decide which of my associates will fail?

William Clement Stone, a Chicago millionaire, in an interview said, "Only if you have drive, the push, 'the want to' will you succeed in any field." He went on to say, "Regardless of your religious beliefs, read the Bible, the most inspirational book of all time. And learn to employ the power of prayer." This man had learned the value of commitment. He had the "want to." He had also learned to turn to God for direction, guidance, and help.

Many people are motivated by spiritual goals. The question is, "For what reasons?" Is it because of good feelings and promised rewards, or is it because of fear of not living the commandments? The best motivation is toward the positive. Total commitment to correct gospel principles brings joy, satisfaction, and the abundant life.

Dale Carnegie once said, "If you are not in the process of becoming the person you want to be, you are automatically engaged in becoming the person you don't want to be."

However, we must realize not all problems of life can be solved at once. A commitment to solve our daily needs and the reaching of immediate lesser goals will bring meaningful successes. Realize that God will judge you by the way you make use of all your possibilities. It is wise and proper to want to make the most of every opportunity, but don't quit or weep because of failure or disappointments. Break down big commitments into smaller ones that you can handle. Then self-esteem will grow and commitment toward goals of greater magnitude will become possible. The journey of success is long and is dotted with a series of commitments to worthy goals. A person does not become committed to worthwhile goals just by making the declaration or decision. It must be daily progression toward established purposes.

When one is wholly committed, added strengths and talents become evident. Assistance comes from unexpected sources. Who of us has not accepted some assignment with fear and trepidation, feeling totally inadequate to take on such a responsibility? But with concern and obedience we move forward—working hard and praying often. As the task is completed, to our surprise, we have been successful. We humbly realize that our own abilities have been added upon.

Goethe wrote, "What you can do, or dream you can, begin it. Boldness has genius, power, and magic in it." (*Faust: Vorspiel auf dem Theater,* 1:227, as translated by John

Anster, *Faustus, A Dramatic Mystery: Prelude at the Theatre,*
1835, 1:303.) We would add that commitment has genius,
power, and magic in it.

The scriptures say it this way: "For I know that the
Lord giveth no commandments unto the children of men,
save he shall prepare a way for them that they may accomplish the thing which he commandeth them." (1 Nephi
3:7.)

A truly committed person does not falter in the face of
adversity. Until one is committed, there is a chance to
hesitate, to go off in another direction, or to be ineffective.
Members within our ranks who are committed to living
the gospel of Jesus Christ will not be affected by the ra-
tionale of hecklers.

Our enemies are becoming more hostile with each passing week. They seem intent not only on deceiving the
uncommitted among us but on leading astray even the
elect. They criticize our leaders. They scoff at what we
consider to be sacred. They mock ordinances and covenants we know to be true and holy. They delight in dis-
covering and sharing human flaws and frailties among our
leaders past and present rather than acknowledging and
benefiting from the truths they taught. They go to the tree,
and instead of enjoying the fruit thereof, they point out
the scars discovered on the tree trunk.

Do not be deceived. God will not be mocked. (See
Galatians 6:7.) We have no intention of quarreling or demanding equal time to refute. We invite the dissenters as
well as all others to open their eyes and see the beauties
and thrills available to those who walk in His path looking
for the good.

For example, it is a sad day in the life of any individual
or group when by present training, attitude, and design,
they would go to a football game and judge the participants
by the dirt and grime on their uniforms rather than by
how many tackles were made or yards gained.

By the same token, where is the pleasure for these same

people who, attending a big-league baseball game, will not cheer or clap for the home-run hitter who drives in the winning runs but would rather dwell upon the fact that when the star, according to their research, was in grade school he was kept after school for misconduct? Woe unto those who feast on the dirt and the distasteful instead of the fruits.

Contrast those attitudes with that demonstrated by an elderly widow acquaintance of ours who travels to the temple every morning, spends the day attending sessions, and returns home by bus tired and worn just because "I love everyone, even those I cannot see." Her attendance record? "I go every day it is open. Sometimes when I don't feel too strong it is difficult, but I make it somehow." The word is *commitment*.

We all have eyes, ears, and minds to lift, lead, and love. Total commitment to God and His ways will not permit us to engage in destructive criticism, retaliation, or undue disgust. We should commit ourselves to marching shoulder to shoulder in the battle to save souls—without destroying, condemning, or belittling.

With Paul's conversion came commitment. Joseph Smith placed commitment ahead of life itself. From the time of his first vision until his martyrdom, he was a victim of bitter persecution, reviling, and ridicule, but never did he falter in spite of extreme adversity. As he recorded his story, he wrote: "It was . . . a fact that I had beheld a vision. I have thought since, that I felt much like Paul, when he made his defense before King Agrippa, and related . . . when he saw a light, and heard a voice; but still there were but few who believed him; some said he was dishonest, others said he was mad; . . . but all this did not destroy the reality of his vision. He had seen a vision, he knew he had. . . .

"So it was with me. I had actually seen a light, and in the midst of that light I saw two Personages, and they did in reality speak to me; and though I was hated and persecuted for saying that I had seen a vision, yet it was true; . . . for I had seen a vision; I knew it, and I knew that God knew it, and I could not deny it, neither dared I do it; at least I knew that by so doing I would offend God, and come under condemnation." (JS–H 124-25.)

Certainly neither the Apostle Paul nor Joseph Smith waivered, though they faced severe trials. As mentioned earlier, in our present day there are many who are sowing seeds of dissension and discord. With half truths and slander, they are endeavoring to lead members of the Church of Jesus Christ into apostasy. Sometimes I wonder just how Christian it is to call someone else un-Christian, when we are referring to his or her conduct. Those who are firmly committed to living the gospel of Jesus Christ will not be confused, confounded, or led astray.

If we profess to be Latter-day Saints, let us be committed to living like Latter-day Saints, using Jesus Christ as our master teacher.

It is not too late to commit ourselves to living the gospel totally while here on earth. Each day we must be committed to lofty Christian performance because commitment to the truths of the gospel of Jesus Christ is essential to our eternal joy and happiness. The time to commit and recommit is now.

I'm thinking of a five-year-old boy who fell out of bed during the night and came crying to his mother's bedside. To her question, "Why did you fall out of bed?" he replied, "I fell out because I wasn't in far enough!"

It has been my experience over the years that, generally speaking, those who fall out of the Church are those who aren't in far enough.

In a simple statement, the difference between those committed and those who are not is the difference between the words *want* and *will*. For example, "I want to pay tithing, but our funds are so limited," or "I will pay my tithing." "I want to go to sacrament meeting if I have time," or "I will go to sacrament meeting." "I would like to be a good teacher, but the children are so noisy," or "I will be a good teacher."

To reap the full benefits of life, we must fill our days with commitment to worthy goals and principles. There is no other way. As these commitments lead us to action, we will find added growth and dimension that will guide us toward a productive life here on earth and open the door for eternal life with our Father in heaven.

The word is *commitment*. To be something, we must be committed. God is our Father. Jesus is our Savior, and this is His church. May we commit ourselves to living Christlike lives regardless of the environment or opposition.

8
Straightway

"He saith unto them, Follow me, and I will make
you fishers of men. And they straightway left
their nets, and followed him."
(Matthew 4:19-20.)

I was once visiting in a faraway country with a discouraged missionary. When I asked,"How long has it
been since you wrote a letter to your mother?" he said,
"Oh, about three or four weeks, I guess." When I sug-
gested he write her a letter straightway, he responded
with, "What does *straightway* mean?"

Straightway is a power word. *Straightway* is an action
word. It means immediately, without delay or hesitation.
It means at once. Also, it is associated with having no
curve or turn—a straight course, track, or path. *Procrastination* would be the very opposite of *straightway*. To procrastinate is to put off intentionally and habitually something that should be done. Procrastination is unproductive
delay. Someone has wisely said, "Procrastination is a silly
thing; it only brings me sorrow. But I can change at any
time; I think I will—tomorrow!"

"Jesus, walking by the sea of Galilee, saw two brethren,
Simon called Peter, and Andrew his brother, casting a net

into the sea: for they were fishers. And he saith unto them, Follow me, and I will make you fishers of men. And they *straightway* left their nets, and followed him.

"And going on from thence, he saw other two brethren, James the son of Zebedee, and John his brother, in a ship with Zebedee their father, mending their nets; and he called them. And they immediately left the ship and their father, and followed him." (Matthew 4:18-22; italics added.)

My remarks today are going to be centered around this key word, *straightway*. "And they straightway left their nets, and followed him." How descriptive, how powerful, how rewarding when properly applied in human conduct.

We invite all to serve the Savior and walk in His paths straightway. There is an urgency for all of us who have this knowledge of His divinity to act upon it without hesitation or delay. The time is now.

Joshua reminds us of the importance of making decisions promptly: "Choose you this day whom ye will serve; . . . but as for me and my house, we will serve the Lord." (Joshua 24:15.) Not tomorrow, not when we get ready, not when it is convenient—but "this day," straightway, choose whom you will serve. He who invites us to follow will always be out in front of us with His Spirit and influence setting the pace. He has charted and marked the course, opened the gates, and shown the way. He has invited us to come unto Him, and the best time to enjoy His companionship is straightway. We can best get on the course and stay on the course by doing as Jesus did—make a total commitment to do the will of His Father.

To straightway follow our Savior requires effort on our part. No longer does He personally walk the earth with us, but He has not left us alone. His guidelines and commandments are always with us if we will study the scriptures. We must learn His will before we can do His will.

A prerequisite for "doing" is goal setting. Actions are preceded by thoughts and planning. All of us must take charge of our own lives. We must evaluate the choices that are open to us, and then we must act positively on our own decision. An old proverb states, "A journey of one thousand miles begins with the first step." The word *straightway* suggests the urgency to take that first step toward any worthy goal.

"If you will that I give unto you a place in the celestial world, you must prepare yourselves by doing the things which I have commanded you and required of you," said the Lord. (D&C 78:7.) To take that first step may require great courage, but somehow possibilities and potential strengths begin to appear once the decision to act positively is made. Unsuspected courage and strength will be given to those who start forward in the right decision.

Peter, a lowly, rough fisherman, took that first step and straightway followed Jesus. Strength upon strength was added to him. He grew from the disciple who denied his Master thrice, to the man who could be intimidated by no one. When he and John were set in the midst of "Annas the high priest, . . . and John, and Alexander, and as many as were of the kingdom of the high priest" (Acts 4:6), Peter boldly declared that salvation comes because of Christ.

"Now when they saw the boldness of Peter and John, and perceived that they were unlearned and ignorant men, they marvelled; and they took knowledge of them, that they had been with Jesus." (Acts 4:13.)

The high priest could have brought great harm to these brethren, but he only dared to command them "not to speak at all nor teach in the name of Jesus.

"But Peter and John answered and said . . . , Whether it be right in the sight of God to hearken unto you more than unto God, judge ye." (Acts 4:18-19.) In the face of threats, these Apostles were given added courage: "And with great power gave the apostles witness of the resurrection of the Lord Jesus: and great grace was upon them all." (Acts 4:33.)

By taking that first step straightway, Peter learned to

be a fisher of men. He identified his goals, and as he moved toward them, he grew in strength, power, and conviction.

How wise and blessed we would be if we eliminated procrastination and made a decision to serve the Lord and accept His invitation to "Come, follow me." (Luke 18:22.) Then when we have identified our goal, may we have the courage to act upon our decision, confident that added strength and power will be given according to our needs as we follow the Good Shepherd.

As we plan to follow the Savior straightway, Satan may try to dissuade us by making the task look impossible, by making us doubt our worthiness or ability. Each is different; each has his or her own strengths.

Peter and Andrew were fishermen. Hence, in speaking in terms of their trade, the Savior said, "I will make you fishers of men." (Matthew 4:19.) To the carpenter, He would say, "I will make you builders of men." To the teachers, "I will make you teachers of men." No person has all the talents. "For all have not every gift given unto them; for there are many gifts, and to every man is given a gift by the Spirit of God. To some is given one, and to some is given another, that all may be profited thereby." (D&C 46:11-12.)

Wishing things were different in our lives, or waiting for a roadblock to be removed or an attitude altered, can cause us to mark time rather than to move forward straightway. William Shakespeare wrote, "Our doubts are traitors, and make us lose the good we oft might win by fearing to attempt." (Measure for Measure, act 1, scene 4, lines 77-79.)

Use your specific talents. Don't procrastinate action while wishing for missing abilities. To those who are inclined to respond with "Not now" or "Not yet" to the invitation to "Come, follow me," may we suggest, with all the love and sincerity we possess, He wants you. He will welcome you straightway regardless of where you have been, where you are now, who you are, or what talents you possess or lack.

Some weeks ago following a stake conference meeting, a man who has been totally inactive for many years approached me with great hesitation and said, "I guess I really don't belong here. My life is a mess." To this I responded, "What difference does that make? Of course you belong here."

Those who continually prefer to stir up waters find that they create only a whirlpool and are carried around in circles rather than progressing straightway.

Can we be servants of our Master rather than critics of those who are trying to serve Him? A servant will look for solutions to problems while procrastinators excuse their inactivity by concentrating on the futility of the problem.

Those whose goal it is to follow the Savior straightway not only look for answers to their own problems but also help others find solutions to life's difficulties. They open their hearts and minds to those who are troubled, ignored, or weary.

Just by listening empathetically, we often can help others find their own solutions. Recently a stake president told me that one of the most sincere thank-yous he had ever received came from a young mother with two children who, under very difficult conditions, was trying diligently to succeed as a single parent. After a lengthy interview, her words of appreciation were simply, "Thank you for listening to me. I think I can face my problems much better now."

Our own progress can be enhanced if we can look for solutions instead of being critical of those around us and blaming external conditions for our lack of progress.

Can we be honest with ourselves and examine the reasons we are not following the Savior straightway? Are we being delayed by criticism of another person's actions or attitude toward us? Has our pride been hurt or our ego bruised? Have we jumped to conclusions without accurate facts?

The Savior admonished, "Have peace one with another." (Mark 9:50.) Peace must first come from within. It flows from the individual to the home, to the community, to the nations, and to the world. This peace can only come as we resist the damaging pastime of passing judgment. In the scriptures we are warned to judge not, that we be not judged. (See 3 Nephi 14:1; Matthew 7:1.) Somehow there seems to be something enticing and intriguing about being a self-appointed judge.

Many years ago I heard a story that I've always remembered. Perhaps I heard it when I was running around as a young barefoot boy.

A poor, old French woman was walking along the banks of the Seine River. On her stooped shoulders was draped a threadbare shawl. Suddenly she stopped, leaned down, picked up something that sparkled brightly in the sunlight, and put it under her shawl. A policeman observed her actions and hurried over to her. In a very gruff voice he said, "Let me see what you are hiding under your shawl!" The old woman drew out from the folds in the shawl a broken piece of glass, saying, "It is only a sharp piece of broken glass. I picked it up so some barefoot boy might not step on it and cut his foot."

The policeman was doing his duty, but he was more than willing to convict the woman of a misdeed before he could learn that she had acted with the nobility of a caring soul.

Yes, erroneous judgments of the actions of our fellowmen may be responsible for our delay in straightway heeding the call of our Savior. By pursuing the teachings of Jesus Christ and living gospel principles, we can put aside the hurts and delays that may have been caused by people around us.

Finally, to move and act straightway in the right direction requires self-discipline and self-restraint.

Many live by the motto Play Now and Pay Later. Some think that if they wait long enough, their problems will go away. But they don't. They must be worked through. Before we can solve our problems and put our lives in order, we must accept full responsibility for our problems.

We often avoid taking action because we tell ourselves that our problem was caused by circumstances or people beyond our control. Therefore, we think we can abdicate our responsibility, and we find ourselves hoping that other people or a change of conditions will solve our difficulties. Rather, it is our responsibility to repent—to change, and to move forward without delay. "Do not procrastinate the day of your repentance." (Alma 34:33.)

How comfortable some of us become as we nestle in the web of procrastination. It is a false haven of rest for those who are content to live without purpose, commitment, or self-discipline.

We must heed the words in Alma: "Behold, this life is the time for men to prepare to meet God; yea, behold the day of this life is the day for men to perform their labors." (Alma 34:32.)

Avoid procrastination. We can say with great accuracy procrastination is an unwholesome blend of doubt and delay. Oft-used words of the Savior such as *ask, seek, knock, go, thrust,* are action words. He would have us use action as we teach and live His principles.

"Enter ye in at the strait gate: for wide is the gate, and broad is the way, that leadeth to destruction, and many there be which go in thereat: because strait is the gate, and narrow is the way, which leadeth unto life, and few there be that find it." (Matthew 7:13-14.)

Do not doubt your abilities. Do not delay your worthy impressions. With God's help, you cannot fail. He will give you the courage to participate in meaningful change and purposeful living. We need to repent, straightway, and trust in His reality and capacity to assist us in knowing the abundant life. He will help us learn to be sensitive to our own needs and to those of others. Those who fear, procrastinate. Those who change for the better show progress straightway and become wiser and stronger. We need to develop the courage to straightway take the first step. We need to remember that children learn to walk only because someone encourages them to take the first step.

May we launch straightway toward setting goals that are gospel oriented, knowing that if we use the talents that are ours—that if we help others, strive for peace, avoid being overly sensitive or overly critical—strength upon strength will be added to our own abilities and we will move straightway toward greater growth, happiness, and eternal joys. Our Master and Savior invites us to straightway embrace His truths and enjoy the warmth of His constant companionship.

We must rise by our own efforts and walk by faith. One of our greatest resources for success and happiness is doing the right thing now. All of us as God's children must be taught that meaningful growth must come from within and not from without. By so doing, we will walk in His paths, lift the arms of the weary and oppressed, give encouragement to our associates, develop individual initiative in governing ourselves, carry our crosses with dignity and purpose, and help all to become fishers of men straightway.

The gospel of Jesus Christ is true. Jesus Christ is our Redeemer and Savior. Happiness and eternal life are available to those who will follow Him straightway.

9
Shake Off the Chains

"Put on the armor of righteousness. Shake off
the chains with which ye are bound, and come
forth out of obscurity, and arise from the dust."
(2 Nephi 1:23.)

Some years ago I had an acquaintance who had allowed himself to become a compulsive user of al-
cohol. He drank before he had dinner, and he would
have what he called a "bracer" before involving himself
in major business decisions. During a routine physical ex-
amination one day, a doctor told him that, for the good of
his health, he should break the drinking habit. When I
asked him what he intended to do, he said, "That's easy.
I'll just change doctors."

Another acquaintance is a lovely, well-educated
woman who has been a very heavy smoker. She now tells
us of a few times she even woke her husband up in the
middle of the night and insisted that he go to an all-night
store to get her a pack of cigarettes. This couple came in
contact with the missionaries, believed their message, and
joined the Church. When she knew she had to quit smok-
ing, the woman almost immediately threw off the chains
of this habit and became free of tobacco addiction.

As I have been rereading the Book of Mormon, following the counsel of President Ezra Taft Benson, our beloved
Prophet, I have been even more impressed with the counsel Father Lehi gave his family shortly before his death.
He pleaded with his sons with these words: "Awake, my
sons; put on the armor of righteousness. Shake off the
chains with which ye are bound, and come forth out of
obscurity, and arise from the dust." (2 Nephi 1:23.)

Those words apply to us today. Who among us hasn't
felt the chains of bad habits? These habits may have
impeded our progress, may have made us forget who we
are, may have destroyed our self-image, may have put our
family life in jeopardy, and may have hindered our ability
to serve our fellow beings and our God. So many of us
tend to say, "This is the way I am. I can't change. I can't
throw off the chains of habit."

Lehi warned his sons to "shake off the chains" because
he knew that chains restrict our mobility, growth, and
happiness. They cause us to become confused and less
able to be guided by God's Spirit. Lehi also reminded his
sons that their new land should "be a land of liberty unto
them; wherefore, they shall never be brought down into
captivity; if so, it shall be because of iniquity." (2 Nephi
1:7.) He could have said, "If so, it shall be because ye have
been bound into captivity by the chains of unrighteous
living." Samuel Johnson wisely shared, "The chains of
habit are too small to be felt until they are too strong to
be broken." (*International Dictionary of Thoughts* [Chicago:
J. G. Ferguson Publishing Company, 1969], p. 348.)

The woman of whom I spoke was able to break the
chains of a bad habit because she became committed to
change. Some of the Lamanites under King Lamoni were
able to break the chains of their iniquities of murder, in-
dolence, and hatred when they were taught by Ammon.
They became even more valiant than the Nephites because
they became committed to righteousness.

Righteous living is a shield, a protector, an insulation,

a strength, a power, a joy, a Christlike trait. Yes, living a life of righteousness is a chainbreaker.

Many of us today are shackled by the restrictive chains of poor habits. We are bound by inferior self-images created by misconduct and indifference. We are chained by an unwillingness to change for the better. Is it any wonder, in our day as it was in Nephi's, that God's pleas are "awake," "listen," "procrastinate no longer," "believe me," "come back," and "seek the straight course"?

Shaking off restrictive chains requires action. They cannot be wished away. A declaration will never break chains. It requires commitment, self-discipline, and work.

Chains weigh heavily on troubled hearts and souls. They relegate us to lives of no purpose or light. They cause us to become confused and to lose the Spirit. We need to arise from the dust and enjoy the fresh air of righteousness. We need to move forward in patience, understanding, love, and never-ending commitment.

Sometimes the chains of arrogance and domination cause priesthood bearers to lose their way and stumble. No man in The Church of Jesus Christ of Latter-day Saints is worthy of his priesthood powers and blessings if he makes unrighteous demands upon his wife or family. God forbid that any man would find satisfaction or comfort in exercising this type of domination. "No power or influence can or ought to be maintained by virtue of the priesthood, only by persuasion, by long-suffering, by gentleness and meekness, and by love unfeigned." (D&C 121:41.)

Let me share some chains I have recently observed in the lives of some friends, chains that are causing misdirection, family destruction, loss of self-respect, and sadness.

I am thinking of a young husband and father who is participating in drug abuse. He stands to lose family, employment, personal pride, and his own life. His cries of "I'm hooked" tug at the soul. The use of cocaine and other drugs causes those involved to become totally chained to their addiction. Those who peddle drugs not only provide chains for others, but shackle themselves with the weights of unrighteousness as well. To those not involved, avoid drugs in any form with all of your might. To those involved, seek help to remove the chains that will drag you down and smother you. Drugs are not a "quick fix." They are a quick exit through a door that too often swings only one way—toward heartache and self-destruction.

Believe me when I tell you that some of the saddest sights I have ever witnessed in my life are people living with drug addiction. They are prisoners within their own bodies. Many feel totally helpless, dependent, and desperate. But none should feel hopeless. Lift those chains and fight back for personal dignity, peace, and purpose. Anyone who tells you drug use is the "fun" way is a liar.

Any judge who allows convicted drug peddlers to go their ways with only light penalties isn't worthy of holding the office.

I am acquainted with a wife and mother who is chained securely at the present time to a life-style of murmuring and criticism. She is the first to point out faults in her husband or to repeat neighborhood gossip. How damaging is a habit that permits fault-finding, character assassination, and the sharing of malicious rumors! Gossip and caustic comments often create chains of contention. These chains may appear to be very small, but what misery and woe they can cause!

"O that ye would awake; awake from a deep sleep, yea, even from the sleep of hell, and shake off the awful chains by which ye are bound, which are the chains which bind the children of men, that they are carried away captive down to the eternal gulf of misery and woe." (2 Nephi 1:13.)

Listen to the words of a friend who understands well the meaning of this scripture, a man who was bound by the chains of indifference. But when he sought God's help and turned to righteous principles, those chains were not only broken, but smashed. This letter was received a few weeks ago.

"I was baptized into the Church in March of 1974. At the time, I was employed in a job that required my having to work on Sundays. This, combined with my lack of strength in the gospel, prevented me from becoming an active and faithful member of the Church. Over the years I neglected my daily study and prayers. Throughout this time in my life I drifted farther and farther from the Church and the teachings of the gospel. This neglect brought disappointment after disappointment to me and my family. I was discouraged and disillusioned, and I lacked self-respect and confidence.

"On the afternoon of April 6, 1986, my wife was scanning through the TV channels in search of something to pass away another lazy Sunday afternoon when she came across the Sunday afternoon session of general conference about to begin. We decided to watch and see what was going on as we had lost complete contact with the Church, and I, frankly, could not have told you who the Prophet was at the time.

"The message I listened to was a gift from my Heavenly Father, one that would turn my life around. The message stayed with me for the next couple of days. I commented to my wife how much better I felt about myself and my relationship with others as a result of simply applying some recommended principles. We have since returned to a faithful and active involvement in our ward."

What a blessing it is to rise from the dust and the chains of indifference.

One may ask, "What must I do to break the chains that bind me and lead me away from the path our Savior would have us follow?" These chains cannot be broken by those who live in lust and self-deceit. They can be broken only by people who are willing to change. We must face up to the hard reality of life that damaging chains are broken only by people of courage and commitment who are willing to struggle and weather the pain.

It is true that some people do not want to change, even though they may say they do. Only you can supply the motivation, and only you can decide to change. The Church, the home, the family, friends, and those professionally trained can aid, support, encourage, empathize, and guide, but the work of change belongs to the person. Most often, it is plain hard work.

To change or break some of our chains even in a small way means to give up some behavior or habits that have been very important to us in the past. Generally this is frightening. Change involves risks. "How will people react and respond to me if I change and am different?" Even if our present way of life is painful and self-destructive, some of us think it serves a purpose, and some become comfortable with it.

Every worthy change means risk—the risk of losing an old and damaging habit for a new and improved way of life. If fear and an unwillingness to take the risk and challenge of the better way of life gain the upper hand, we will not be able to change.

Even the chains of fear can be broken by those who will humbly seek God's help and strength. It can be done with this strengthening promise in Doctrine and Covenants 122:4: "Because of thy righteousness . . . thy God shall stand by thee forever and ever."

A truly wise person will constantly move forward, striving for self-improvement, knowing that daily repentance is needed for progress. He or she will realize that the good life is simply conforming to a standard of right and justice. The joys of happiness can be realized only by living lofty principles.

Those who are committed to improvement break chains by having the courage to try. Those who live without commitment mistakenly think it is easier to adapt their lifestyles to the weight and restrictions of chains rather than to put forth the effort to change.

God help us to shake off and break the chains with which we are bound. With God's help they can be shaken off by faith, works, prayer, constant commitment, and self-discipline.

10

I Am An Adult Now

"When I was a child, I spake as a child, I
understood as a child, I thought as a child: but
when I became a man, I put away childish
things."

(1 Corinthians 13:11.)

S ome weeks ago a man holding a high office in the
Church asked a special favor of me. "Would you be
good enough to take the time to listen while a
mother, father, and their teenage daughter, special friends
of mine, try to talk to each other?"

As the four of us sat together, it immediately became
obvious that all channels of communication were jammed
with prejudice, threats, accusations, and resentment. As
the verbal storms developed with bitter intensity, I found
myself the only listener. Even though they had individually
and collectively agreed I would be the counselor, judge,
arbiter, or referee, if you please, I found myself waiting
patiently for an opportunity to be heard. During the heated
and emotional confrontation, the teenager repeatedly expressed her resentment with, "You can't talk to me like
that. I am an adult now. You can't treat me like that. I am
an adult now. You can't dominate my life anymore. I am
an adult now."

Each time she said, "I am an adult now," I cringed. By definition an adult is a person who has attained the age of maturity . . . full grown. While it is true a person may be legally classified as an adult when he or she reaches a certain age, for our purposes today the kind of adult status we are talking about must be earned by actions and attitude.

I am not quite sure who has the right or responsibility to declare someone an adult, but I am quite certain that often the least qualified to make the declaration could be the individual himself. If a person is mature, he or she will not need to announce it. Personal conduct is the only true measurement of maturity. Adult classification when it pertains to behavior does not come with age, wrinkles, or gray hair. Perhaps it is not too far off the mark to say adult conduct is a process. Mature conduct is generally developed through self-discipline, resilience, and continuing effort.

In fairness to the teenager, even though her declaration of "I am an adult now" didn't impress me favorably, there were times during the visit when I thought she showed more maturity than others in the room. When we who are more senior use an expression like "I am older than you" to clinch a point, I am not too sure it is very effective. How much better it is to gain respect and love through worthy parental conduct than to seek it through the means of the age differential.

Young men and young women worldwide, you as well as your parents need not announce or proclaim your maturity. By your faith and works you will be known for what you are. By your fruits you will be known and classified. Those among us who use abusive arguments, temper tantrums, demeaning and painful criticism, fruitless counter-complaints, and disrespect will benefit no one. Let us put away petty malice, resentment, and retaliatory practices that are self-destructive and return to a path of safety well-marked by the Good Shepherd. It takes courage to flee from verbal contention. When maturity begins to set in, adult lives set in. "Let all bitterness, and wrath, and anger, and clamour, and evil speaking, be put away from you, with all malice: and be ye kind one to another, tender-hearted, forgiving one another, even as God for Christ's sake hath forgiven you." (Ephesians 4:31-32.) It is alarming how many older people go through life without ever becoming real adults.

For many years I have had a very vivid picture in my mind of Jesus Christ standing before Pilate. While Jesus stood in front of an angry mob, who sneered and condemned, Pilate tried to get Him to respond and retaliate. He tried to get Him to declare Himself a king. Jesus was silent. His life was His sermon. He was perfect in character, a worthy son, the Only Begotten of the Father. His maturity, if you please, would speak for itself.

"Jesus stood before the governor: and the governor asked him, saying, Art thou the King of the Jews? And Jesus said unto him, Thou sayest. And when he was accused of the chief priests and elders, he answered nothing. Then said Pilate unto him, Hearest thou not how many things they witness against thee? And he answered him to never a word; insomuch that the governor marvelled greatly." (Matthew 27:11-14.)

There are many opportunities to acquire mature behavior in the organizations in the Church. The other day a charming teenager paid a deserving tribute to her Young Women's teacher: "From her example and good lessons, we learned the importance of good grooming. We learned that though each of us is different, each is equally important. She taught us to solve our differences by discussion, not by shouting."

The success of the Scouting program is that it teaches boys to stay on the trail. Boulders and hills don't stop the hike to the top of the mountain. Top awards are not given unless the difficult merit badges are earned as well as the easier ones. The boys' tenacity to continue on the Scouting path, not the honors awarded, is the maturing element of the program.

"A certain man had two sons: And the younger said to his father, Father, give me the portion of goods that falleth to me [I am an adult now] and he divided unto them his living." The parable of the prodigal son is well known to all of us. He left and wasted his substance with riotous living. "When he came to himself he said, . . . I will arise and go to my father, and will say unto him, Father, I have sinned against heaven, and before thee, and am no more worthy to be called thy son: [But I am more of an adult now]. . . . And he arose, and came to his father. . . . His father saw him, and had compassion, and ran, and fell on his neck, and kissed him." I believe it appropriate to say the father too had become more mature during the separation. Think, too, of the maturing and the becoming more of an adult on the part of the elder son when he witnessed and participated in the Christ-like example of his father. (See Luke 15:11-32.)

There is no doubt in my mind that one of the primary reasons Laman and Lemuel murmured and spoke harsh words to their brother Nephi and smote him with a rod was because they were older and more adult than Nephi, so they supposed. Can't you just hear Laman saying, "Nephi, you can't treat me like that. I am an adult now." Nephi displayed real maturity when he declared to his father, "I will go and do the things which the Lord hath commanded, for I know that the Lord giveth no commandments unto the children of men, save he shall prepare a way for them that they may accomplish the thing which he commandeth them." Nephi later recorded, "When my father had heard these words he was exceeding glad, for he knew that I had been blessed of the Lord." (1 Nephi 3:7-8.) Lehi was adult enough to know which son was the most mature and who would be blessed of the Lord accordingly.

Too many of us fail to realize that adult conduct is a process, not a status. To become a disciple of Jesus Christ we must continue in righteousness and in His word. When someone shares with enthusiasm his or her joy in now being an active member of the Church, the thought crosses my mind, "Wonderful, but for how long will you stay that way?" Incidentally, some years ago I was contacted by an insurance agent. When he started his sales approach with "I am an active member of the Church," the first thought that crossed my mind was, "Who said so?"

When someone overcomes the drug habit, and thankfully many have, less time should be spent on announcing the present status and more on staying away from bad habits. Those who are morally clean will conduct themselves in a more adult fashion if they will spend less time declaring it and more time living and teaching others the blessings of chastity. Full-tithe payers will receive more joy and reward from being obedient to the principle of tithing than from being so classified or recommended.

Some will chide and belittle leaders and students of higher education for participating in code-of-conduct guidelines, but those appropriately involved in the wholesome process of mature behavioral discipline welcome the environment. Responsible student conduct on any campus is applauded. A pledge of "on my honor I will do my best," either in writing or when self-enforced, can make the difference in character development. Making and keeping commitments may seem restrictive and outdated in today's world where "play it loose" is the pattern, but the benefits are clear to the mature.

Those who are immature resent counseling or having to report in. They may feel that such interviews are juvenile. Those who strive for continual growth realize that counselors can help them analyze themselves and find solutions to personal problems. In our church, counselors are a source of strength for the Prophet as well as for all of us.

Beware of those seeking excuses for conduct with "I am an adult now. You can't treat me like that." Moral maturity and scholastic maturity must be blended to produce a truly adult person. A commitment to improve daily should be a high priority in the lives of those who would move in the right direction.

There is real purpose and power in the First Presidency's continuing invitation to all Church members to come back. Strength, growth, and happiness result from analyzing the direction our lives are taking. Those who have been lost, misunderstood, or offended, and those totally involved in the Church, are invited to come and fellowship together within the framework of the gospel of Jesus Christ. To be a member of The Church of Jesus Christ of Latter-day Saints is not enough. Participation in Priesthood, Relief Society, Young Women, Young Men, Primary, and Sunday School opportunities is necessary if we are to move forward anxiously in personal development that is adult, real, and eternal. Perhaps all of us would do well to realize that as we promote personal activity and involvement in the Church, it might be much better to be classified a member of "good coming" instead of a member in good standing. It is our responsibility and privilege to encourage the immature and give them opportunities for growth and development.

Joseph Smith declared to the world that he was like a rough stone shaped and polished by the stream of life. Bumps, disappointments, and the unexpected helped him gain the status of being wise beyond his years. Oftentimes maturity can best be measured by our endurance. "If the heavens gather blackness, and all the elements combine to hedge up the way; and above all, if the very jaws of hell shall gape open the mouth wide after thee, know thou, my son, that all these things shall give thee experience, and shall be for thy good. The Son of Man hath descended below them all. Art thou greater than he?" (D&C 122:7-8.)

My young friends, in a spirit of love I suggest that we avoid the placing of self-labels. For you to be classified all-state, all-American, or even all-world doesn't mean anything if you alone determine the winner and present the trophy to yourself. By the same token, who among us has the right to label himself or herself as a loser, no good, a dropout, or a failure? Self-judgment in any direction is a hazardous pastime. It is a fact of life that the direction in which we are moving is more important than where we are. I have never heard the best-educated ever declare, "I am educated now." Some of the most potentially wise people in the world forfeit that classification when they spend their time advertising their abilities and knowledge rather than using their wisdom to improve themselves and help those with whom they associate.

Mothers, fathers, and family members, maturity does not necessarily come with age. Let us communicate in words and deeds our concern and love for each other. Threats, ears that do not hear, eyes that do not see, and hearts that do not feel will never bring joy, unity, and growth. Patience with others, self, and God bring eternal maturity. Let God and our daily actions determine the authenticity of the statement "I am an adult now."

11
Holding the Priesthood, A Sacred Trust

"No man taketh this honour unto himself, but he that is called of God, as was Aaron."
(Hebrews 5:4.)

It was sixty long days after my twelfth birthday before I was ordained a deacon. I say "long" because most of my boyfriends in other wards were being ordained on or very near their twelfth birthdays. I hadn't asked but wondered why my bishop was so slow in getting to something as important as this.

When the day finally came, the bishop said, "I want you to know being ordained a deacon doesn't come at a certain time, day, or month. It comes when those in authority think you're ready. Time is not the determining factor." I think I could have said rightfully and respectfully to the bishop, "I was just as ready sixty days ago as I am now," but I didn't. My life was in order. I couldn't understand the delay. This good bishop was teaching me a great lesson, and I have always tried to remember it. Priesthood possession and power do not come at a certain date or time. They should be extended when the one having authority feels it is the right time.

This important learning experience taught so many years ago has helped me in counseling members of the Church worldwide. When they ask, "How long before I can hold the Aaronic Priesthood?" or "When can I be ordained an elder?" or "How many years do I have to wait before I can have my priesthood blessings restored?" I am better prepared to respond.

Holding the priesthood is a sacred trust. Sharing the priesthood with family and friends is a God-given right and responsibility. Holding the priesthood is as permanent as we are worthy. How proud I was to be a deacon and pass the sacrament in a similar manner to the way Jesus Christ broke the bread and blessed it and passed it to His apostles. When the Council of the Twelve and the First Presidency meet in the temple on special occasions and partake of the sacrament, I am honored, humbled, and thrilled when I am assigned to pass the sacrament. Even though I have been ordained an apostle, I am proud I am still a deacon and can exercise that power that is mine. I am pleased also to be a teacher, a priest, and an elder. If I live worthily, these offices will always be my priceless possessions.

When I became a deacons quorum president, I learned I had a serious responsibility to assist others in their attendance and in carrying out their assignments. I and others in my quorum now had the power and authority to act. I soon realized that when you take someone else to the quorum meeting, you get there too. Hands had been laid upon our heads. We had memorized the Articles of Faith, but now the fifth article, "We believe that a man must be called of God, by prophecy, and by the laying on of hands by those who are in authority, to preach the Gospel and administer in the ordinances thereof," had new meaning. Also having additional significance was the scripture "And no man taketh this honour unto himself, but he that is called of God, as was Aaron." (Hebrews 5:4.)

President Joseph F. Smith described with clarity and

beauty the important features of the priesthood in the Church when he said: "[The priesthood] is nothing more nor less than the power of God delegated to man by which man can act in the earth for the salvation of the human family, in the name of the Father and the Son and the Holy Ghost, and act legitimately; not assuming that authority, nor borrowing it from generations that are dead and gone, but authority that has been given in this day in which we live by ministering angels and spirits from above, direct from the presence of Almighty God." (*Gospel Doctrine*, 5th ed. [Salt Lake City: Deseret Book Company, 1939], pp. 139-40.)

The mighty priesthood of God was delegated to Adam and passed on down to Abraham, who received it from the great high priest, Melchizedek, "which priesthood continueth in the church of God in all generations and is without beginning of days or end of years. And the Lord confirmed a priesthood also upon Aaron and his seed, throughout all their generations, which priesthood also continueth and abideth forever with the priesthood which is after the holiest order of God.

"And this greater priesthood administereth the gospel and holdeth the key of the mysteries of the kingdom, even the key of the knowledge of God. Therefore, in the ordinances thereof, the power of godliness is manifest. And without the ordinances thereof, and the authority of the priesthood, the power of godliness is not manifest unto men in the flesh." (D&C 84:17-21.)

The priesthood can bring glorious gifts, powers, and responsibilities that are beyond measure. Those who would honor the sacred trust of holding the priesthood will need to be firm in the right to represent the Most High here upon the earth. Upon this trust and power is God's earthly kingdom dependent.

"Hearken, O ye people of my church, saith the voice of him who dwells on high, and whose eyes are upon all men; yea, verily I say: Hearken ye people from afar; and ye that are upon the islands of the sea, listen together. For verily the voice of the Lord is unto all men, and there is none to escape; and there is no eye that shall not see, neither ear that shall not hear, neither heart that shall not be penetrated." (D&C 1:1-2.)

We holders of the priesthood, as Joseph Smith, are given keys and powers to build the kingdom of God through a delegation of authority that is most rewarding.

Some years ago President Marion G. Romney had an eye operation. The day following his surgery I was visiting with his secretary and asked if she thought it would be appropriate and timely for me to visit him in the hospital. When she indicated it would not only be possible but, she thought, welcomed by President Romney, I made my way to his room. When I looked at him, I noticed that most of his head and both eyes were covered with bandages. As he lay quietly, it was difficult to tell whether he was asleep or resting. I decided to sit quietly at the side of his bed for a few minutes. Before too long a nurse came into the room and, recognizing me, said, "Hello, Elder Ashton, how are you?" When I responded to her greeting with "I am fine. How is President Romney?" she said, "Let me tell him you are here." She touched his arm gently and said, "Elder Ashton is here. Would you like him to give you a blessing?" Even though President Romney was weak and under heavy sedation, I will never forget his reply when in a frail but firm voice he said, "No, I don't want Elder Ashton to give me a blessing. My home teachers gave me a blessing last night."

Here this member of the First Presidency who could have called upon any of his associates to give him a blessing realized that according to pattern and recommendation his own home teachers not only had the right but the power to bless him at his invitation. To say that I was impressed with this is an understatement. The power of the priesthood is greater than an individual or his calling.

What a blessing it is for us to have the power to place

our hands upon the sick and the afflicted and extend to them appropriate, comforting, and rewarding promises as directed by the Spirit. This is possible only through people who have the authority and live to honor it. A father who bears the priesthood of God is never released from his responsibilities. He may release himself through sin, but his is an eternal calling. We need to not only honor our priesthood but be worthy to carry it with dignity, pride, and effectiveness. In the ninth chapter of Acts, verse 6, the Savior was asked, "Lord, what wilt thou have me do?" And an appropriate answer comes from the Book of Mormon, 3 Nephi, chapter 27, verse 27: "Therefore, what manner of men ought ye to be? Verily I say unto you, even as I am."

Hopefully the priesthood of God will help us to be better individuals as we remember that Jesus Christ is the way, the light, and the truth. We become even as He is as we love Him, keep His commandments, and walk in His paths. Studying scriptures and knowing Him, His life, and His example are stepping stones to becoming more like He is. We need to walk in His steps. Our priesthood can be an anchor. No one can come back into the presence of our Father except through Him.

We should not only honor the priesthood but respect those who are worthy bearers of the priesthood and who live close to their Heavenly Father. I had the occasion to have minor surgery during the past six months. What a joy, a strength, and a comfort it was to have our two sons come into our home with their wives and with my wife Norma at their side giving me a blessing before I underwent the operation. To have this priesthood power in our family and to have those close to us exercising it in a proper way is a reward in and of itself. When my sons were deacons, teachers, and priests, we had taught them of the restoration of the priesthood and its availability to them if they would live worthily. Now they were exercising their priesthood powers in extending a blessing to their father.

What a joy it has been over the years to have a sweet-
heart and wife who, when there has been a special need,
would quietly say, "Marv, will you please give me a blessing? Then I know everything will be all right." These tender
moments of exercising and sharing the priesthood cause
me to thank God for His trust.

Besides being a sacred power, the priesthood gives one
the right and the authority to act, which includes to lead,
to heal, to bless, to bind, to set in order, to organize, to
bear special witness, to home teach, to baptize, to confirm,
and to perform other God-given obligations, duties, and
spiritual pleasures. To carry out God's purposes and while
so doing prove themselves, it is necessary for boys and
men in the Church to work under the direction of His
authorized servants. There is a great strength provided
from associations with others who are seeking and fulfilling
similar goals and service opportunities.

Priesthood makes a great brotherhood possible and
most desirable. To illustrate this, I should like to share a
story related by Elder Henry D. Taylor, a General Authority
associate of mine who passed away recently. I heard him
give a talk at General Conference that he titled "Man Does
Not Stand Alone."

In that talk he said, "A boy was extended an invitation
to visit his uncle who was a lumberjack up in the North-
west. . . . [As he arrived] his uncle met him at the depot,
and as the two pursued their way to the lumber camp, the
boy was impressed by the enormous size of the trees on
every hand. There was a gigantic tree which he observed
standing all alone on the top of a small hill. The boy, full
of awe, called out excitedly, 'Uncle George, look at that
big tree! It will make a lot of good lumber, won't it?'

"Uncle George slowly shook his head, then replied,
'No, son, that tree will not make a lot of good lumber. It
might make a lot of lumber but not a lot of *good* lumber.
When a tree grows off by itself, too many branches grow
on it. Those branches produce knots when the tree is cut

into lumber. The best lumber comes from trees that grow together in groves. The trees also grow taller and straighter when they grow together.' "

Then Brother Taylor made this observation: "It is so with people. We become better individuals, more useful timber, when we grow together rather than alone." (*Conference Report,* April 1965, pp. 54-55.)

I naturally related to this illustration because I spent all my life prior to becoming a General Authority in businesses related to the products of the tree. I love trees. Over the years I have learned what makes good trees and good boys.

> The tree that never had to fight
> for sun and sky and air and light,
> but stood out in the open plain
> and always had its share of rain,
> never became a forest king
> but lived and died a scrubby thing.
> The man who never had to fight,
> who never had to win his share
> of sun and sky and air and light,
> never became a manly man
> but lived and died as he began.
> Good timber does not grow in ease,
> the stronger the wind,
> the tougher the trees.
> (Author unknown)

In this same trend of thought President David O. McKay said on another occasion, while addressing the general priesthood of the Church, "Fellow presiding officers in missions, stakes, wards, and quorums, make your quorums more effective in regard to brotherhood and service. The quorums are units which should effectively hold the priesthood in sacred bonds and in helpfulness.

"I refer particularly to the senior members of the Aaronic Priesthood—you businessmen, successful in the business world; you professional men who have devoted

your time to the success of your vocations and are successful and are leading men in civic and political affairs —
get together more closely in your quorum . . . and help
one another. If one of your number be sick, two or three
of you get together and call on him. . . .

"You elders perhaps have one of your number sick,
and his crop needs harvesting. Get together and harvest
it. One of your members has a son on a mission, and his
funds are getting low. Just ask if you can be of help to
him. Your thoughtfulness he will never forget. Such acts
as these are what the Savior had in mind when He said,
'Inasmuch as ye do it unto the least of these my brethren,
ye do it unto me.' (See Matthew 25:40.)" (*Conference Report*,
October 1955, p. 129.)

In this important day our beloved President Ezra Taft
Benson and his noble counselors Gordon B. Hinckley and
Thomas S. Monson have extended a warm and caring invitation to come back and share the joys of Church activity
and priesthood involvement.

The power, strength, and importance of the priesthood
is reinforced by a statement made by President Stephen L
Richards, former counselor in the First Presidency. He said:
"I have reached the conclusion in my own mind that no
man, however great his intellectual attainments, however
vast and far-reaching his service may be, arrives at the full
measure of his sonship and the manhood the Lord intended him to have, without the investiture of the Holy
Priesthood, and with that appreciation, my brethren, I
have given thanks to the Lord all my life for this marvelous
blessing which has come to me — a blessing that some of
my progenitors had, and a blessing which more than any
other heritage I want my sons and my grandsons and my
great-grandsons to enjoy." (*Conference Report*, October
1955, p. 88.)

I humbly thank my eternal father for the special priesthood calling and responsibility that is now mine. When
President Joseph Fielding Smith and his counselors called

me to be a special witness, an apostle, and a member of the Quorum of the Twelve, it was the most humbling experience of my life. How rewarding and comforting it was when Harold B. Lee, who ordained and set me apart at the request of President Smith, promised greater powers and greater measures of the spirit to help me to function as a priesthood leader.

The power and authority to act for and in behalf of God is upon the earth. I bear witness to the deacons, as well as to those called to other offices within the Aaronic and Melchizedek Priesthood, that you have a power that is real and priceless. We should humbly thank God daily for the restoration of the priesthood. Our priesthood responsibilities can help us in our personal lives, homes, families, and leadership positions. We do not boast. We know we are weak, but with God's help and the priesthood many mighty works can be accomplished, as pointed out in Alma 26:10-12: "When Ammon had said these words, his brother Aaron rebuked him, saying: Ammon, I fear that thy joy doth carry thee away unto boasting.

"But Ammon said unto him: I do not boast in my own strength, nor in my own wisdom; but behold my joy is full, yea, my heart is brim with joy, and I will rejoice in my God. Yea, I know that I am nothing; as to my strength I am weak; therefore I will not boast of myself, but I will boast of my God, for in his strength I can do all things; yea, behold, many mighty miracles we have wrought in this land, for which we will praise his name forever."

God help us to be worthy. God help us to be appreciative of the restored priesthood we bear and share. God help us as Aaronic and Melchizedek Priesthood holders to be true to ourselves and our Eternal Father.

12
Peace: A Triumph of Principles

"He who doeth the works of righteousness shall
receive his reward, even peace in this world,
and eternal life in the world to come."
(D&C 59:23.)

Many years ago I heard a story that impressed me.
A beautiful little blind girl was sitting on the lap
of her father in a crowded compartment in a
train. A friend seated nearby said to the father, "Let me
give you a little rest," and he reached over and took the
little girl on his lap.

A few moments later the father said to her, "Do you
know who is holding you?"

"No," she replied, "but you do."

Some might be inclined to say, "What a perfect trust
this child had in her father." Others may say, "What a
wonderful example of love." And still others might say,
"What an example of faith." To me it indicates a beautiful
blending of all of these principles, which brought a priceless inner peace to the child. She knew she was safe because
she knew her father *knew* who was holding her. Affection,
respect, and care over the years had placed in this little
girl's heart a peace that surpasseth all understanding. She
was at peace because she knew and trusted her father.

We plead for peace in our prayers and thoughts. Where is peace? Can we ever enjoy this great gift while wars, rumors of wars, discord, evil, and contention swirl all around us? The answer is yes. Just as the little blind girl sat on the stranger's lap with perfect contentment because her father knew him, so we can learn to know our Father and find inner peace as we live His principles.

It is very significant that when Jesus came forth from the tomb and appeared to His disciples, His first greeting was, "Peace be unto you." (Luke 24:36.) Peace — not passion, not personal possessions, not personal accomplishments nor happiness — is one of the greatest blessings we can receive. Our trust and our relationship with our Heavenly Father should be one similar to that of the little blind girl and her earthly father. When sorrow, tragedy, and heartbreaks occur in our lives, wouldn't it be comforting if when the whisperings of God say, "Do you know why this has happened to you?" we could have the peace of mind to answer "No, but you do."

Certainly peace is the opposite of fear. Peace is a blessing that comes to those who trust in God. It is established through individual righteousness. True personal peace comes about through eternal vigilance and constant righteous efforts. No one can be at peace who is untrue to his or her better self. No one can have lasting peace who is living a lie. Peace can never come to the transgressor of the law. Commitment to God's laws is the basis for peace. Peace is something we earn. It is not a gift. Rather, it is a possession earned by those who love God and work to achieve the blessings of peace. It is not a written document. It is something that must come from within.

The Salt Lake Valley was settled by those who trekked over the plains under extremely difficult conditions so they could worship God in peace. Left behind was Nauvoo, a deserted city desecrated by the uninformed, misinformed, embittered enemies of the Church. Peace had flown from the City Beautiful. What a price some of those who have gone before us have paid for the privilege of worshipping in peace.

Never will peace and hatred be able to abide in the same soul. Permanent peace will elude those individuals or groups whose objective is to condemn, discredit, rail at, or tear down those whose beliefs are different from their own. These people live by hatred and would destroy others insofar as it is in their power to do so. True Christians have no time for contention. Lasting peace cannot be built while we are reviling or hating others. Those who preach hate, ridicule, and untruths cannot be classified as peacemakers. Until they repent they will reap the harvest to which those engaged in the business of hatred are entitled. Feelings of enmity and malice can never be compatible with feelings of peace.

"The wicked are like the troubled sea, when it cannot rest, whose waters cast up mire and dirt. There is no peace, saith my God, to the wicked." (Isaiah 57:20-21.)

However, only those at peace can properly cope with accusations and slander. Inner peace is the prized possession of God's valiant. A testimony of the truthfulness of the teachings of our Savior gives personal peace in times of adversity.

There are those who dangle false enticements of peace before us. These are they who are greedy and power hungry. "Be not deceived; God is not mocked: . . . He that soweth to his flesh shall of the flesh reap corruption." (Galatians 6:7-8.) Inner peace flees from those who sacrifice virtue for sexual promiscuity. There are some who advocate and promote new sexual exploits under the guise of "relief from stress." These people are only sowing unto the flesh and peddling devilish deeds. Wickedness, no matter how it is labeled or camouflaged, will eventually bring grief and heartache and wipe out inner peace.

Peace will never be the possession of those who participate in vulgar conversations and behavior. Let us not be planters of poisonous seeds. Rather let us nourish roots of peace in the soil of righteous principles.

It was Ralph Waldo Emerson who declared the mighty truth "Nothing can bring you peace but yourself. Nothing can bring you peace but a triumph of principles." ("Self-Reliance," in *Ralph Waldo Emerson: Essays and Lectures* [New York: The Library of America, 1983], p. 282.)

Peace is not a purchase away. Peace is not when the final installment is paid. Peace is not when marriage comes nor when all the children are enrolled in school. Peace is not when the last child returns from the mission field. Peace is not when an inheritance is received. Peace is not when the scars of death start to heal.

True peace must not be dependent upon conditions or happenings. Peace must stem from an inward contentment built upon trust, faith, and goodwill toward God, others, and self. It must be constantly nurtured by the individual who is soundly anchored to the gospel of Jesus Christ. Only then can a person realize that the trials and tribulations of daily life are less important than God's total goodness.

Lasting peace is an eternal personal quest. Peace does come from obedience to the law. Peace comes to those who develop character and trust.

We have a young grandson who loves gymnastics. He is progressing well and delights in showing us what he can do. While he develops these performance skills his body is maturing in limberness and strength. The last time he invited me to feel the muscles in his arms, I congratulated him. I was proud. As he jumped away from me (gymnasts, it seems, are always jumping and springing), I was impressed with the thought that his parents, grandparents, teachers, and others have an obligation to teach him one of life's great truths: flabbiness of character should always be more of a concern than flabbiness of muscles. Body-building and body-conditioning are worthwhile goals, but more is needed to gain true inner peace. We must blend balance in our lives and increase in wisdom and stature, and in favor with God and man (see Luke 2:52) to reach our full potential.

No peace will be lasting unless it is built upon the solid foundation of eternal principles such as love of God, love of neighbor, and love of self. Those who love their neighbors can bring peace and happiness to many. Love can build bridges to understanding and tear down walls of suspicion and hate. Christlike love can bring peace into any neighborhood. With that kind of love each of us can help resolve petty differences, be they in the home or the community.

While living in another nation just before World War II was to begin, a leading government official had been working hard to maintain peace for his country. He had in his hands a signed document guaranteeing peace. After negotiating in good faith, he seemingly had achieved that for which millions of his fellow citizens had been hoping and praying. He publicly assured all of us that the document meant peace for our times.

Soon, however, he realized that he had been deceived. Those with whom he had negotiated were selfish, greedy, and power hungry. They were only bargaining for time to solidify their position. War came.

We learned that peace can never be achieved when we deal with those who deceive and who ignore the basic principles taught by our Savior.

At such times external events make it even more imperative that we seek peace within ourselves. It is futile to seek it from outward sources.

It was George C. Marshall who wisely said, "We must take the nations of the world as they are, the human passions and prejudices of people as they exist, and find some way to secure . . . a peaceful world."

Peace must be a triumph of principles. Selfishness and lack of patience seem to block the way. We cry out today with urgency, "Have mercy, O Lord, upon all the nations of the earth; have mercy upon the rulers of our land; may those principles, which were so honorably and nobly defended, namely, the Constitution of our land, by our fathers, be established forever." (D&C 109:54.) The respected Winston Churchill once said, "The day will come when . . . victorious nations will plan and build in justice and freedom a house of many mansions, where there will be room for all."

We would pray earnestly today that all leaders of nations, large and small, free or oppressed, would know: "Above all things, clothe yourselves with the bond of charity, as with a mantle, which is the bond of perfectness and peace." (D&C 88:125.)

Despite the challenges of curbing federal budget deficits and riots and terrorism, of controlling the arms race and inflation, and of winning an ambitious battle for tax reform, thank God America is at peace. Thank God for those other nations who teach and live in peace. Thank God for worthy people who work to keep it that way. Our responsibility as a nation and its people is to continue to take the lead in furthering peace on earth and goodwill toward all. (See Luke 2:14.) To all people worldwide who would anxiously engage themselves in lasting peace, we share: "But learn that he who doeth the works of righteousness shall receive his reward, even peace in this world, and eternal life in the world to come." (D&C 59:23.)

The individual, the home, the church, the school, the government are the fundamental institutions upon which lasting peace depends. The main purpose of schools must always be to develop character, to develop loyalty to the government, loyalty to the home, and loyalty to the individual. This is what real peace is all about—internal and external. No peace, even though temporarily achieved, will be lasting unless it is built upon the solid foundation of such eternal principles as love of God, love of neighbor, love of self. Most people yearn for peace, cry for peace, pray for peace, and work for peace, but there will not be lasting peace until all humanity follow the path pointed out and walked by the living Christ. There can be no peace in sin and disobedience. If I do not have peace within me, others around me will suffer.

God has a special love for those of His children who promote and advocate peace. Our responsibility as Church members is to instill in an ever-growing number of people the fact that our personal attitudes and behavior can bring a measure of peace to our troubled world and a sense of stability to anxious times. With peace in our hearts we can know that the trends of the world and the criticisms of men cannot alter the truths of God.

When we properly blend into our lives true principles of love, honesty, respect, character, faith, and patience, peace will become our priceless possession. Peace is a triumph of correct principles.

Just as the little girl could sit peacefully on the stranger's lap because her father knew him, so we can find peace if we know our Father and learn to live by His principles.

None of us will avoid the storms of life. The winds and the waves will periodically interfere with our chosen course. But the laws of the gospel can bring us back on course and guide us to peaceful waters.

13
Courage for Christmas

"Be strong and of a good courage, fear not, nor be afraid . . . for the Lord thy God, he it is that doth go with thee; he will not fail thee, nor forsake thee."

(Deuteronomy 31:6.)

A lovely woman who had lost her companion through death once told me, "I wish I could say I am looking forward to the holidays, but without Richard, Christmas is going to be very difficult this year."

With this heartfelt comment, and knowing the anguish and loneliness resulting from separation from one so close, I can understand how some wish the holidays were not so difficult. The loss of a loved one is oftentimes cruelly related to the holiday season.

Such situations prompt me to extend the gift of courage for Christmas to all. Courage makes it possible for memories and present pleasantries to overshadow past losses and loneliness. The spirit of giving, sharing, and praising can prevail over anxiety and loss when courage fills our lives. With courage, we can take from Christmas the true gifts available and make them part of a season intended to be uplifting and glorious.

Christmas is intended to be a joyous time, a time for all to reflect upon the fact that the Lord has come. We have the opportunity to repeat and share the joyous news of the birth of the child Jesus, our Savior, Friend, and Redeemer. We are beneficiaries of His priceless gift: His life, His example, His love, and His redeeming grace.

I could wish for nothing more for my friends, associates, and family members alike than that they would accept the gift of courage for Christmas — the courage to be Christlike; the courage to be childlike in faith, in belief, and in joy, anticipated and real; the courage to be honest with God, with self, and with all humanity; and the courage to place others ahead of themselves. How wonderful it is when we have the courage to declare, without hesitation and with real conviction, "Him only shall I serve." (See Luke 4:8.) How rewarding it is when we solemnly declare that the birth of Jesus is real, significant, and an eternal blessing for all mankind. In this spirit we learn to share rather than to "wish well" in our daily pursuits.

Courage is the capacity and the ability to decide before anything else is really decided, to predetermine to move forward joyously in our worthy pursuits. Courage conquers all things. Courage is the desire, the strength, the composure, the determination, the drive, the sustaining power, and the love to properly relate and respond. Courage is the power to meet all that life has to offer. Courage enables us to see ourselves and our own situation in a proper light and to share with others in a meaningful way.

We cannot walk through life on mountain peaks. There are rivers and valleys along the way, and some are deep and treacherous. Some are cruel and challenging to human endurance. Some rivers and valleys would have us lose our way, and some mountain peaks would have us bask in self-sufficiency. All of these ultimately result in heartache, distress, and frustration.

Illness, death, disappointment, and discouragement, as well as honor, wealth, and public acclaim, often require great courage to ensure proper survival. Courage is that ingredient in life which makes it possible for us to anticipate and prepare ahead for whatever comes. How great, how wise, how strong are those who realize that with God's help we can accomplish all things!

I would like to share five gifts of courage for Christmas, with the hope that one or more can be helpful for each of our Christmases, present and future.

1. *The courage to choose.*

"Choose you this day whom ye will serve, . . . but as for me and my house, we will serve the Lord." (Joshua 24:15.) We need to make honest decisions. We need the courage to stand up and be counted. We need the courage to choose the right and let the consequences follow.

What a powerful example for strength and enduring faith we have in the life of our Savior:

> Then was Jesus led up of the Spirit into the wilderness to be tempted of the devil. And when he had fasted forty days and forty nights, he was afterward an hungred. And when the tempter came to him, he said, If thou be the Son of God, command that these stones be made bread. But he answered and said, It is written, Man shall not live by bread alone, but by every word that proceedeth out of the mouth of God. . . . Jesus said unto him, It is written again, Thou shalt not tempt the Lord thy God. . . . Then saith Jesus unto him, Get thee hence, Satan: for it is written, Thou shalt worship the Lord thy God, and him only shalt thou serve. (Matthew 4:1-4, 7, 10.)

Jesus chose appropriately. He chose to remain firm. He chose to carry out His earthly mission and maintain a proper relationship with His Heavenly Father. How important it is for us to have the courage to choose wisely when choices are placed before us! To choose right over the convenient, the popular, or the socially accepted way is a sign of strength. We need courage to choose change over conflict and inner anguish. We need courage to choose to repent rather than rebel. Such decisions give each of us the opportunity to grow, to rededicate, to recommit, and to restructure our life.

In the mission field I once met a young woman who had been a member of the Church for three years and who had been serving as a full-time missionary for three months. "How is your missionary life going?" I asked. "Quite well," she said. I could tell by her tone that perhaps she wanted to say more, so I said, "Share with me. Why do you report 'quite well' instead of 'very well'?" She replied, "Sometimes my heart aches when I look back and realize what a decisive choice I had to make." When I probed further, she told me this story:

"I had to make a choice between membership in The Church of Jesus Christ of Latter-day Saints and my mother's continuing love. My testimony and the conviction of my heart and mind told me the Church was true and that I must accept it. When I went to my mother and shared with her my desires and feelings, she told me, 'If you join the Mormon Church, just remember you don't have a mother anymore.' Elder Ashton, it wasn't easy for me to say to my mother, 'I must join the Church. It is true, and I cannot deny it. I hope, Mother, that this will not be your decision, but if I must choose, I must choose the Church.' " Then she concluded, "It is not a pleasant and happy situation to be without a mother, but I know that with God's help I will win her back."

Not many of us must choose between church and parents. We have to admire a person who not only has joined the Church, accepted it fully, and is now sharing with others, but who also has the courage, after having made this important choice, to say, "I know that with God's help I will win my mother back."

The courage to choose and to make decisions based upon fact, feelings, and promptings, regardless of the reaction or responses of others, is a God-given virtue that makes life meaningful and worthwhile.

In today's society it often takes extreme courage to choose Jesus Christ to be our best friend and Savior when others would try to convince us that He doesn't even exist, that He doesn't know us, that He doesn't care. It takes courage to share His life, His ways, and His peace when others about us would cause confusion.

Yes, I would give courage for Christmas, even the courage to choose properly, with strength, fortitude, and conviction, when a choice is placed before us. We need to think, to ponder, and to pray when we make a decision, and then have the courage to choose the right and accept the consequences without hesitation or fear.

2. *The courage to continue.*

We need the courage to remain true and faithful, to show by our life-style day after day that we are not ashamed of the gospel of Jesus Christ. We need courage so that regardless of environmental pressures or situations, we will continue worthily in the pursuit of lofty goals in His paths. We need to follow the admonition of the scriptures: "Be ye doers of the word." (James 1:22.)

President Spencer W. Kimball's life will always be an example for all to follow when we think of the courage to continue. He met all of life's challenges physically, socially, financially, and spiritually with a firm determination to continue. He is an outstanding example of continuing when others of lesser stature and commitment would be inclined to fall by the wayside. Certainly it is accurate to say that his courage was greater than his strength. He was strong because he was courageous. He knew no other way to live.

It is important to have the courage to continue when some enemies along the sidelines of life would threaten, belittle, misrepresent, and cause us to miss a step with their slander, falsehoods, and misinterpretations. We should never allow our enemies to cause us to lose ground or direction by their comments, accusations, contention, or innuendoes. There is no time for contention. Proper courage will keep us moving onward and upward regardless of situations along life's path. We need the courage to continually bear our own witness of the Savior of mankind. He lives. Though He suffered for our salvation and for our redemption, He continued courageously because He moved forward without hesitation in His Father's business.

3. *The courage to carry our cross.*

No matter what size, shape, or weight, we should each carry with dignity our cross of burden, tragedy, or success. God will help us bear it. We all have crosses to bear. Some crosses are unseen. Some cause us to become weary with the weight and the responsibility. Sometimes the heaviest cross to shoulder is to share in the load of another's burdens. When this is properly understood, no cross can be considered light.

Our responsibility is to do more than bear our cross. We need to bear our cross and move ahead without hesitation. Proper courage makes this possible. What strength and direction we should receive when we read that Jesus "bearing his cross went forth." (John 19:17.) He not only bore His cross, but He "went forth." We have the same responsibility. We have the same opportunity not only to bear our cross, but to keep moving without becoming weary. Jesus told His disciples, "If any man will come after me, let him deny himself, and take up his cross, and follow me." (Matthew 16:24.) In this powerful scripture we learn that carrying the cross is not sufficient. We have the responsibility not only to carry the cross, but to follow Him as we make our way. Each of us, in our struggle to carry our cross, will need constant encouragement to follow as we go forth.

Our Savior, Jesus Christ, left no reason for doubt as to His feelings regarding those who are unwilling to bear the cross and follow Him. He said, "He that taketh not his cross, and followeth after me, is not worthy of me. He that findeth his life shall lose it: and he that loseth his life for my sake shall find it." (Matthew 10:38-39.) A cross can be a strength in helping us to find the real purpose of life and its meaning. Particularly is this true as we not only carry our cross but also share the burdens of others, as we lose our lives in serving and lifting others. If we want to be His disciples, we must bear His cross and be near Him, for He has said, "Whosoever doth not bear his cross, and come after me, cannot be my disciple." (Luke 14:27.) Bearing the cross and coming after Him makes it possible for us to be one with Him.

Crosses have many configurations; they have different weights, edges, and lengths. All require strength if the load is to be carried appropriately. We cannot always unburden ourselves of the cross we have been given, but we can rid ourselves of the weight we need not carry.

Some crosses are self-inflicted; some we unknowingly place upon ourselves. Oftentimes a cross, even though it is heavy, is allowed to become comfortable. With proper attitude and commitment, such crosses can be lifted.

We should not allow our own stupidity to cause us to stagger or trip with the loads we carry. We should rid ourselves of prejudices and weaknesses that make staggering or lost direction acceptable in our path. We can carry our crosses well if we but seek His help and His strength to supplement our own. I recall a blind man's reaction to a dedicatory service in the Jordan River Temple in Salt Lake City. He described the temple as being "beautiful, totally and completely." His cross made it possible for him to see the temple through spiritual eyes and feelings that were significant and pleasing not only to him but also to those of us with whom he shared his impressions.

Sometimes our cross, as we carry it, gives us a new outlook and a new eternal dimension. As Joseph Smith was imprisoned in jail at Liberty, Missouri, the Lord told him, "Know thou, my son, that all these things shall give thee experience, and shall be for thy good. The Son of Man hath descended below them all. Art thou greater than he?"

(D&C 122:7-8.) Jesus Christ carried the cross for all of us in making salvation and eternal life real. A cross carried courageously will make it possible for us to be stronger than had we been free of the burden.

4. *The courage to be clean.*

All of our thoughts, remarks, dress, grooming, and daily activities should be pursued in the realm of the clean life. We should be selective in the books, magazines, movies, television shows, and personal conversations available to us, and we should avoid those associations that are not uplifting. We plant seeds before we harvest. Unclean thoughts result in unclean deeds, and unclean deeds bring unclean lives. We have been admonished: "Be ye clean that bear the vessels of the Lord." (D&C 38:42.)

The courage to be clean in our attitudes and in our thought processes is so important because thoughts beget behavior. Much of the music that people listen to today can degrade and cause improper actions and reactions. When we allow the words, the beat, and the environment to result in low thoughts and poor performance, we are unfair with ourselves. No greater sermon in fewer words has ever been shared on this subject than "Be ye clean." God help us to be clean in thought, clean in act, and clean in appearance.

5. *The courage to communicate properly.*

Courage is needed if we are to properly counsel, confide, comfort, and console. To ponder, to meditate, to show sincere concern, to pray, and to teach prayer are such important aspects of communication. The courage to communicate good cheer, to communicate peace, and to communicate the great joys of the gospel of Jesus Christ, as well as to communicate love, affection, warmth, and happiness, are so greatly needed today. The courage to bring tidings of great joy, the courage to share a warm handshake, a smile, a nod of the head, a wink of the eye, a good word, and sincere pleasantries — all are powerful methods of communication.

We need to continually take the time to communicate with our Heavenly Father and those about us. As we share, we can make the difference in the life and light of others. We lift as we love and as we convey our love through communication. In the scriptures we read, "But to do good and to communicate forget not: for with such sacrifices God is well pleased." (Hebrews 13:16.)

In all of our relationships, communication should be open, comforting, and sincere. God has invited us to communicate with Him through prayer continually, no matter where we are or what the circumstances. He wants to hear from us. He loves us. He knows us. He wants to be part of our lives and to help us solve our problems. How important it is to improve our communication with Him and with others every day!

The Lord's Prayer is still a worthy model of communication in content, approach, and attitude:

> After this manner therefore pray ye: Our Father which art in heaven, Hallowed be thy name. Thy kingdom come. Thy will be done in earth, as it is in heaven. Give us this day our daily bread. And forgive us our debts, as we forgive our debtors. And lead us not into temptation, but deliver us from evil: For thine is the kingdom, and the power, and the glory, for ever. Amen. (Matthew 6:9-13.)

Family members often cry for the strength that accompanies good communication. Some are awkward and hesitant in developing the channels that make two-way dialogue possible. Wise mothers and fathers will communicate more effectively with each other and will, in turn, teach their children and others in the process. What a blessing is a warm personality, properly communicated, as we go down life's paths with others!

May God help us to give and to share courage for Christmas by having the courage to choose, the courage to continue, the courage to carry our cross, the courage to be clean, and the courage to communicate.

At this Christmas season I extend to you the gift of courage. I pray that our Heavenly Father will help you and me in receiving this priceless gift. May He help us to share it as we seek to make it a permanent possession, and may He help us to have the courage to know, to believe, and to declare that Jesus is the Christ, the Lord of lords, the King of kings, our Savior born in Bethlehem in humble surroundings and circumstances.

We need the continuing courage to declare to the world that Jesus lives today, that He is our Savior, our Friend, the Son of God, and that His church and kingdom are available to all today. God does live. Jesus is one with the Father. It takes courage not only to know but also to declare these truths. With courage as a permanent possession, all of these things are possible, and they will bring peace and joy to each of us as we know and understand the real meaning of Christmas. Courage makes it possible for cherished memories and mountains to overshadow losses and valleys in our quest for the joyous.

Index